Contents

Foreword by Alex Quigley
Introduction

Part I. How all teachers can be teachers of literacy

1. Closing the attainment gap through curriculum and pedagogy 15

Part II. Creating classrooms where disadvantaged learners thrive: best practice within the subject disciplines

2. English literature 45
3. English language 57
4. Maths 69
5. Science 79
6. History 87
7. Geography 93
8. Religious studies 101
9. Expressive arts 107
10. Technology and related subjects 111
11. Media studies 113
12. Physical education 119
13. Modern foreign languages 121

Part III. Whole-school approaches to improving literacy

14. Explicit vocabulary teaching and the TA Dictionary 127
15. Staff development 153
16. Building a reading and writing culture 161
17. From a whole-school approach to a personalised approach 189

Acknowledgements 197

Foreword

Literacy matters.

You will find very few teachers, if any, who dispute the importance of every student being able to read and write with skill and fluency. Literacy matters to life chances and to school success. And yet, crucially, many teachers of science, or geography, or history, or business studies, or art, and even English, can lack the confidence to address literacy barriers and to best manage students' needs in their subject domain.

The ways in which we talk, read and write in each academic discipline are well-known by teachers in secondary schools, but the nuanced subject-specific strategies to explicitly teach talk, reading and writing in each discipline too often go untaught and can prove commonly misunderstood. Whole-school literacy sessions share issues and strategies with the very best of intentions, but then teachers return to their classroom and can struggle to marry these generalised approaches to the highly specific ways that you read a maths problem, or write a scientific report, or read a poem, in their subject discipline.

Literacy matters but, too often, how we approach literacy runs aground because it is not adequately tailored to the demands of the academic subject.

So, what are we to do? It is not a matter of ignoring decades of effort and research, or throwing the proverbial literacy baby out with the bathwater. It is a case of carefully recalibrating our approach to literacy. By focusing on 'disciplinary literacy', we offer teachers a crucial bridge between general knowledge of literacy and the practical implications for thinking, reading, writing and talking like a subject expert in history, biology or mathematics.

Disciplinary literacy matters because it offers the subtle and vital knowledge that subject teachers need to adapt their practice. It meets teachers where they are. It combines the disciplinary knowing with the doing.

That is not to say this hasn't been tried before, or that it proves easy work. Despite lots of accessible research evidence attending disciplinary literacy, too often teachers struggle to apply that research in practical terms to their work in the classroom. Happily, Kathrine Mortimore has produced a teacher-friendly account of disciplinary literacy that is stuffed full of useful worked examples and subject-specific perspectives to help teachers transform their work.

Disciplinary literacy matters. And it matters to every teacher and pupil. Indeed, success in each and every classroom depends upon it.

Alex Quigley, author of *Closing the Vocabulary Gap*
and *Closing the Reading Gap*

To Justin – thank you for being the spark.

For Annelise and Xanthe.

'For to all those who have, more will be given, and they will have abundance; but for those who have nothing even what they have will be taken away'

MATTHEW 25:29

Introduction

When you have been a teacher for a number of years, becoming a student again is a humbling experience. This is particularly true when one of your teachers is Geoff Barton, the former head who is now general secretary of the Association of School and College Leaders. Back in 2012, I was fortunate enough to sit in a classroom and listen to him talk about a topic that was gaining increasing national focus and attention: educational attainment inequality, its causes and, more importantly, what could be done about it. Literacy was at the heart of this challenge. His book *Don't Call it Literacy!*[1] was an important and practical guide to the whole school community working together to ensure that young people had the tools necessary to access the curriculum.

Geoff's lecture stayed with me and I made the focus of my dissertation research for my master's degree this fundamental question of educational inequality. I was fascinated by the idea of the 'Matthew effect', the term coined by Robert K Merton to refer to the cumulative advantage gained by more senior scientists, and then appropriated by Keith E Stanovich within his research into reading ability. In a similar vein to the theory put forward by ED Hirsch Jr,[2] Stanovich[3] referred to the compounding nature of disadvantage within the school environment. He argued that an attainment gap in literacy is likely to equate to an attainment gap across the board, with the 'word rich' getting richer and the 'word poor' becoming poorer. It has been encouraging to see how this research has become deeply ingrained in the educational landscape over

1. Barton, G. (2012) *Don't Call it Literacy! What every teacher needs to know about speaking, listening, reading and writing*, Routledge
2. Hirsch Jr, ED. (1996) *The Schools We Need and Why We Don't Have Them*, Doubleday
3. Stanovich, KE. (1986) 'Matthew effects in reading: some consequences of individual differences in the acquisition of literacy', *Reading Research Quarterly*, 21:4, pp.360-407

the past decade, with schools devoting more and more focus and energy to tackling educational inequality and this phenomenon of cumulative disadvantage.

Despite this focus and energy, however, educational inequalities still pervade our schools, with outcomes for disadvantaged students continuing to fall behind the rest of the school community. There are many issues surrounding the definition of 'disadvantaged' – it remains a controversial term that is not always helpful in identifying those young people in greatest need. Although schools understandably place emphasis on this headline measure, it makes more sense to carry out a detailed analysis of the individual needs of all children within a school setting (discussed in greater detail in chapters 16 and 17), alongside deploying those teaching methods likely to have the greatest impact on learning (discussed further in chapter 1).

So, although this book has 'literacy' within the title, I am not going to lecture all teachers that they must endlessly check their students' spelling, punctuation and grammar. I am not going to implore all teachers to shoehorn the reading of complex texts into every lesson, or ask them to make sure that extended writing features frequently when the central focus is actually for students to develop their skill and competence in catering, construction or composing music.

Instead, I am going to approach disciplinary literacy according to what decades of research shows us good teaching looks like within each subject. I am going to set out the ways in which those students who are most behind academically, as a result of their literacy skills, can be brought forward by every teacher in the school community. It is my firm belief that when a child begins secondary school with below age-related reading ability, we can work together to equip them with the literacy skills they need in order to attain vital qualifications and become fully functioning members of society.

Alongside this, I will address the perennial conflict within secondary schools between literacy leaders and teachers of subjects from which students are extracted in order to participate in literacy interventions. Although educationalists agree that literacy is important, it is often seen as a skill prioritised at the expense of all else; some teachers feel their subjects have been squeezed out of the curriculum in favour of an 'obsession' with English. Add to this the prioritisation of maths and subsequent numeracy interventions and it is no wonder that many teachers resent the disruption to their lessons for something that is already prioritised. The problem is that these skills are not always prioritised effectively. Interventions can become disruptive to the teacher who is attempting to deliver an already squeezed curriculum, and to the student who feels cheated out of taking part in subjects they feel they can be successful in.

This book offers ways to resolve this conflict by reducing the need for intervention altogether. Although some children will need specific one-to-one phonics instruction, for example, literacy skills can and should be developed throughout their curriculum experience. This does not look the same in every subject. In fact, many whole-school approaches to literacy are unhelpful in achieving this aim, as teachers are devoting lesson time to activities they know are not fundamentally useful for improving children's literacy skills *or* their competence within the particular subject. I will set out ways to empower teachers to get on with doing what works within their subject, in a manner that will facilitate a child's success across the curriculum.

Part I

How all teachers can be teachers of literacy

Chapter 1. Closing the attainment gap through curriculum and pedagogy

What is 'low literacy'?

Before discussing the practical steps that can be taken to support children with lower literacy competence, I need to explain how I am defining this term. Various methods of testing literacy ability are set out in chapter 16; essentially, these return a reading age and a standardised age score. The standardised age score is useful in determining those children who are most behind in their literacy levels, as it takes into account their precise age and also how other children nationally have performed on the same test. Just as GCSE results can be represented on a bell curve, the standardised age score organises student results in the same way.

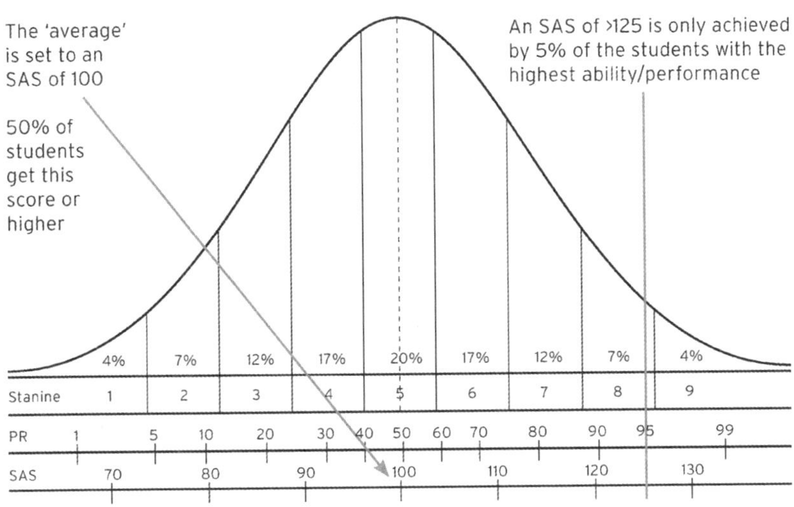

This bell curve is organised into 'stanines'. The children in stanine 1 are those who are most likely to need very personalised intervention. The children in stanines 2-4 are those who will not necessarily need one-to-one intervention, but will benefit from a school culture of disciplinary literacy. Of course, every child will need effective screening to determine their literacy needs when they first arrive at secondary school, and regular monitoring will be necessary in order to identify those who do not make progress and then decide on an appropriate course of action. This is why I have felt it important to include a chapter on personalised approaches: chapter 17 considers how to support children who have special educational needs that affect their literacy ability.

It *is* possible to provide personalised support for children in classrooms that adopt the most effective teaching strategies. This book sets out to join the dots between the growing body of evidence within cognitive science relating to what makes effective teaching, the argument for a knowledge-rich curriculum and the requirement to improve literacy skills. These three things are inextricably linked and together can provide the antidote to the cumulative disadvantage phenomenon. Schools that adopt this approach will benefit disadvantaged children disproportionately while not disadvantaging those who are already achieving well. Effectively, this approach levels the playing field for all children, ensuring that, as far as possible, factors beyond their control no longer determine their life chances.

Effective practice in developing disciplinary literacy

The Education Endowment Foundation (EEF) usefully visualises disciplinary literacy as a tree with wide-ranging branches.[4] The trunk of the tree represents the foundation of effective literacy instruction; the branches reflect the way in which this takes different directions within different disciplines. In this chapter, we will explore this central

4. Quigley, A and Coleman, R. (2019) *Improving Literacy in Secondary Schools: guidance report*, Education Endowment Foundation. Retrieved from: https://educationendowmentfoundation.org.uk/public/files/Publications/Literacy/EEF_KS3_KS4_LITERACY_GUIDANCE.pdf (accessed 19.09.20)

foundation; in Part II, we will take each subject in turn and consider the variety of directions that effective disciplinary literacy can take.

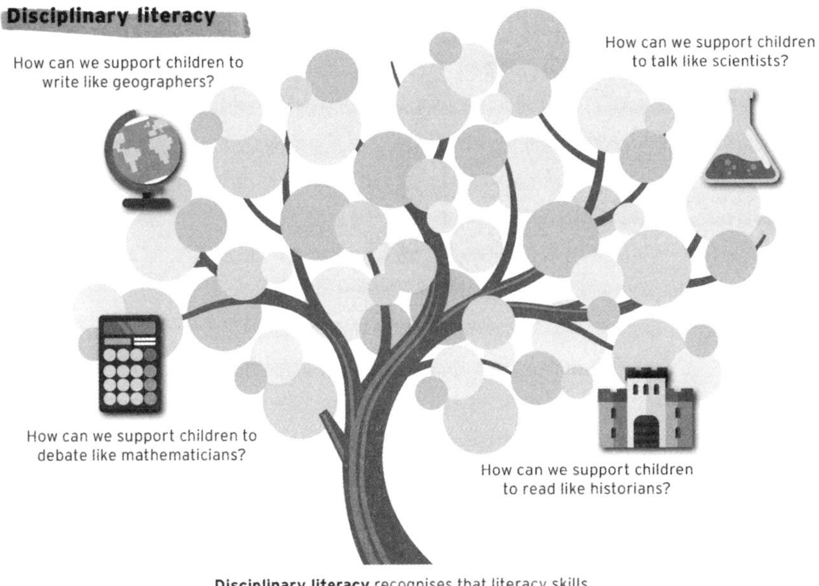

Adapted from source: Education Endowment Foundation

In order to fully explore what constitutes the 'trunk' of the tree in terms of literacy instruction, it is important to first consider what makes effective teaching, particularly for those children who are furthest behind in their literacy competence. To do this, it is helpful to take a step back in a child's reading journey and look at research aimed at our colleagues in primary schools. Hollis S Scarborough's reading rope[5] is an excellent visual representation of the elements of skilled reading ability.

5. Scarborough, HS. (2001) 'Connecting early language and literacy to later reading (dis)abilities: evidence, theory, and practice', in Neuman, SB and Dickinson, DK (eds), *Handbook of Early Literacy Research*, Guilford Press, pp.97-110

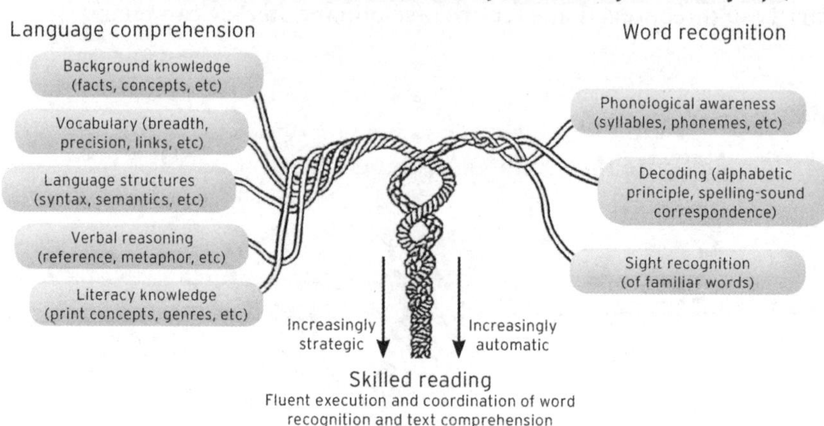

Adapted from source: Scarborough, 2001

By the time children reach secondary school, the vast majority will have mastered the 'word recognition' strands of the rope. Careful diagnosis when they first arrive with us should determine if that is not the case and specialist intervention should be provided (see chapters 16 and 17). For many children, it is not that they do not possess the individual strands of the rope, rather that they are not at the point where the strands are tightly woven together. These children need to build their stamina and fluency through the regular practice of reading so that, as with any other skill, it becomes increasingly automatic. They will benefit the most from a school culture that gives them regular opportunities to read. As the EEF has identified, the factor that is likely to have the most impact on their reading ability is being offered opportunities to read in all subjects where appropriate.

For the majority of children who have low literacy skills on arrival at secondary school, the 'language comprehension' strands of the Scarborough reading rope are those where strong focus and attention are required from all their teachers. This focus on language comprehension needs to be supported by a solid foundation of good teaching in all subjects. This essentially forms the basis of disciplinary literacy.

There are two questions that excellent teachers ask themselves before they begin planning a curriculum and teaching their subject:

- Do I have a crystal-clear idea of the **core knowledge** that my students will need in order to be successful in my subject?
- Do I have a crystal-clear idea of how my students will need to **demonstrate their skill and competence** in order to be successful in my subject?

These two key areas could be likened to Scarborough's reading rope, with a child needing to master each individual strand of knowledge before weaving them together to demonstrate their skill and competence. In a blog post, Alex Quigley writes about this process as it relates to constructing an essay, and the separate strands that are needed in order to 'train an essay writer' who can weave them together.[6]

There has been a raging and often unhelpful debate that sets up a false dichotomy between knowledge and skills. Although it is fair to say that each has been almost fetishised at points, neglecting one in preference for the other is unlikely to result in students, particularly our most disadvantaged students, making good progress. If a child spends all their time learning facts and information but never has a chance to put this into practice, they are unlikely to achieve the highest possible marks. They may well feel confident tackling short-answer questions, but they may drop marks when it comes to extended answers that require them to jump through what often feel like arbitrary hoops in order to demonstrate assessment objectives. Daisy Christodoulou articulates this exceptionally well in her book *Making Good Progress?*[7] She refers to the 'knowing-doing gap', whereby a child knows that they should, for example, start a sentence with a capital letter, but often does not apply this knowledge to their writing. Christodoulou persuasively argues that the best way to close this gap is through the deliberate-practice method – the 'isolation and practice of the particular subskill one wants pupils to be able to do'.

6. Quigley, A. (2017) 'How to train a GCSE essay writer'. Retrieved from: www.theconfidentteacher.com/2017/04/how-to-train-a-gcse-essay-writer-part-2 (accessed 19.09.20)
7. Christodoulou, D. (2017) *Making Good Progress? The future of Assessment for Learning*, OUP

One of the most common misconceptions of schools that promote a knowledge-rich curriculum is that they are environments in which children focus purely on learning information by rote, without ever being given the opportunity to develop their skills within a subject. Nothing could be further from the truth, as a key aspect of learning a piece of information is developing the ability to apply this knowledge in a variety of contexts. Circling back over key knowledge and re-applying it are central to the knowledge-rich approach.

Knowledge and skills are the two key strands of great teaching, but they are also the two key strands of disciplinary literacy. In order to be literate within a particular subject discipline, students need to be able to express their knowledge of that subject in a manner appropriate to the discipline. This looks different in different subjects, as we will explore in Part II. Some subjects require students to have a strong agility in applying procedural knowledge to questions that then allow them to carry out complex calculations, often in innovative ways (once we reach pure mathematics at A-level, for example). Other subjects require a strong foundation of conceptual knowledge demonstrated through building up a portfolio of individual responses to that knowledge; as in the expressive arts, this can result in experimentation with different styles that allow students to reveal part of themselves and their human experience.

In his essay 'The curriculum as the cause of failure',[8] Siegfried Engelmann argues for a strong relationship between knowledge acquisition and pedagogical approaches to acquiring competence within a subject. I want, at this point, to express my gratitude to those educators who are furthering the link between research and evidence-based approaches to learning within the classroom. *The researchED Guide to Explicit and Direct Instruction*,[9] edited by Adam Boxer and series editor Tom Bennett, has been infinitely useful in putting this chapter together, as has Tom

8. Engelmann, S. (1993) 'The curriculum as the cause of failure', *The Oregon Conference Monograph*, 5, pp.3-8. Retrieved from: www.zigsite.com/PDFs/Curriculumascauseoffailurepdffinal.pdf (accessed 19.09.20)
9. Boxer, A (ed). (2019) *The researchED Guide to Explicit and Direct Instruction*, John Catt

Sherrington and Oliver Caviglioli's *Teaching Walkthrus*,[10] which presents the ideas of Engelmann and Barak Rosenshine in a digestible format. I recommend these books as a means of developing a broader appreciation of evidence-based classroom approaches. This chapter sets out how these approaches have particular relevance to literacy.

Developing a secure knowledge base

A child is not going to be able to read a complex text, write an extended piece of writing or articulate their ideas orally if they do not have the key knowledge required to access that task. If we refer again to the Scarborough reading rope (page 18), an essential strand in developing language comprehension is background knowledge. This fact is so often ignored when it comes to improving reading ages and when viewing English in particular as a 'skills-based' subject. What is also frequently not taken into account is the importance of a knowledge-based curriculum in developing literacy competence. Peter Johnston explores at length the effect of prior knowledge on reading comprehension tests, and the resulting bias owing to varying levels of background knowledge.[11] The infamous 'dodo' KS2 SATs paper of 2016 highlighted this issue to our primary colleagues and reinforced arguments that access to a broad and balanced curriculum is key to developing overall reading ability.

As a way of illustrating the relationship between reading comprehension and background knowledge in a secondary context, I have undertaken a review of all of the English language exam papers set by AQA since the new specifications in 2016. The full details of this can be found in chapter 7, but essentially I found that out of the 12 papers set, eight drew upon key knowledge of geography. For example, in one paper the story is about a couple who are in the Pyrenean mountains when an avalanche occurs. A child with an awareness of the hazards of a mountainous environment will be better placed to predict the dangers that await the protagonists

10. Sherrington, T and Caviglioli, O. (2020) *Teaching Walkthrus*, John Catt
11. Johnston, P. (1984) 'Prior knowledge and reading comprehension test bias', *Reading Research Quarterly*, 19:2, pp.219-239

as they read the calm and peaceful opening. This illustrates how central a broad and balanced knowledge-based curriculum is to all children's ability to access the texts presented in the English language exams. But, more than this, the power of the interplay of knowledge between one subject and another cannot be underestimated, particularly when it comes to reading comprehension. A secure knowledge base developed within history will have knock-on benefits when teaching art, for example.

The influence on UK education policy of Hirsch's work, particularly his book *The Schools We Need and Why We Don't Have Them*,[12] is explained by Nick Gibb in an essay collection[13] published by Policy Exchange in 2015 to explore the relationship between knowledge and curriculum, and the associated benefits and challenges. In his essay, Gibb outlines the lack of specificity within the 2007 curriculum that he inherited as schools minister in 2010 – for example, the lack of references to geographical places or historical events that were to be studied. Knowledge was seen as a means to acquiring skills, and there was a resistance to attributing 'value' to some knowledge over other knowledge. The government sought to change this and the national curriculum of 2013 set out a programme of study in the spirit of Hirsch. This resulted in widespread assessment reform that significantly increased the body of knowledge young people were expected to learn in their GCSE and A-level study. These sweeping changes were met with mixed responses from the teaching profession, and were viewed by some as 'right wing' and 'elitist'.

In the same collection of Policy Exchange essays, Michael Fordham describes this opposition and why it is misguided:

> '*The argument is that knowledge is value-laden and dangerous and that any attempt to teach knowledge to pupils is indoctrination. What Hirsch and other traditionalists show us is that the contrary is the case: it is by immersing ourselves in prior traditions – of which*

12. Hirsch Jr, ED. (1996) *The Schools We Need and Why We Don't Have Them*, Doubleday
13. Simons, J and Porter, N (eds). (2015) *Knowledge and the Curriculum: a collection of essays to accompany ED Hirsch's lecture at Policy Exchange*. Retrieved from: https://policyexchange.org.uk/wp-content/uploads/2016/09/knowledge-and-the-curriculum.pdf (accessed 19.09.20)

> *the academic disciplines represent the best means available to use for studying the natural and social world we share – that we are able to enter into meaningful conversations about those traditions and how they might be extended in the future. Education in the academic disciplines is liberating in that it sets us free, but it does so not by getting us to stand empty-headed on an Archimedean point from which we might challenge dominant narratives, but rather by climbing inside the traditions of the past, and thus entering into the great conversations of mankind. A secondary school curriculum that does not focus on academic knowledge does not prepare children for these conversations and this is why, contrary to the progressive line of argument, it is traditionalism that can claim the moral high ground in preparing children for citizenship in a democratic society.'*

Part II of this book focuses on each subject in turn and its value in terms of the disciplinary knowledge it offers young people the opportunity to engage with, thus allowing them to enter the 'great conversations'. Those with weaker literacy skills are those in greatest need of this knowledge to support their understanding of the texts they encounter across the curriculum and their ability to engage with reading for pleasure. In order to set the cumulative disadvantage phenomenon into reverse, we need to remove the barriers that a lack of background knowledge presents to children who struggle to access the curriculum.

Katharine Birbalsingh had no doubt about the centrality of a knowledge-based curriculum when establishing her free school in North London, which opened its doors to students in 2014 with the mantra 'knowledge is power'. I visited Michaela Community School in 2015 and that visit had a profound impact on my thinking. It was a privilege to see Jo Facer teaching English to a class whose level of engagement was beyond anything I had witnessed before, and I was fortunate to discuss with her the booklets she had devised alongside her team. I saw Jonathan Porter reading a novel with his tutor group, and I was shown by several students how knowledge organisers were used in relation to homework and classwork. I listened to a whole year group reciting *Invictus* with passion and enthusiasm before they were given a topical issue to discuss over lunch; I was seated with a group of students who invited me into their discussion. If you wish to see how a school community can come together to create an environment that gives children every opportunity to improve their literacy skills, I would recommend you visit Michaela.

Knowledge organisers and retrieval practice

The main purpose of my visit to Michaela was to see how knowledge organisers worked in relation to homework, as I had been tasked with reviewing my school's homework policy. As explained by former Michaela deputy head Joe Kirby on his blog,[14] students receive knowledge organisers for each topic they are studying. Their homework is to learn this key conceptual knowledge and vocabulary, and they are tested on it in class. At Michaela, teachers use students' performance on the test to determine whether they have completed the appropriate study, or if they need to study further after school in the form of a detention. The principle behind this aligns with the school ethos: knowledge is power. On my visit, it was clear that the students themselves were behind this idea and understood that it was not good enough to simply copy out chunks of information – they must learn it in order to demonstrate that their homework is complete.

At Michaela, there is a strong relationship between the key facts learned during independent study, the low-stakes quizzing that happens in each lesson and the curriculum. It sounds straightforward, but it was surprising how disconnected these things were when my school first introduced knowledge organisers. Whereas staff at Michaela created their curriculum from scratch in the context of a brand new school, it was much more challenging to implement knowledge organisers in an existing context with units of work already in place in Years 7-13. For us, it was a time of great flux in terms of curriculum: new specifications at GCSE and our desire to raise the level of challenge at KS3. Of course, the curriculum needs to be right first of all, with teachers having a strong sense of what they want students

14. Kirby, J. (2015) 'Knowledge organisers'. Retrieved from: https://pragmaticreform.wordpress.com/2015/03/28/knowledge-organisers (accessed 19.09.20)

to know. For many years, I would teach a novel with a very wide sense of all the contextual knowledge and thematic interpretations I wanted to convey. Pinning down the powerful knowledge that would allow students to be most successful, and putting in place frameworks for them to circle over that knowledge (and vocabulary), was revolutionary. In Michaela's most recent book,[15] Katie Ashford discusses the pitfalls that schools across the country have faced when introducing knowledge organisers; I will address how to avoid some of these pitfalls later in this chapter.

Knowledge does not exist in isolation: the clear grasp of one concept provides fertile ground for another, and even those students who often lack confidence in trying out new ideas are better placed to do this if they have been successful in remembering key information. Retrieval activities can be carefully aligned to ensure that key concepts are foregrounded in previous units of work, and misconceptions are identified and straightened out before the lesson that builds on this conceptual knowledge takes place. This is particularly powerful for those with weaker literacy skills, who have the opportunity to experience some 'pre-teaching' of the vocabulary and concepts that are vital to the lesson. It can be easy to assume that because a concept has been taught once and apparently understood, it will be recalled when it relates to a new topic. Equally, it can be easy to assume that those with weaker literacy skills will never learn particular concepts because they are too challenging. But carefully sequenced retrieval practice, supported through homework, can ensure that students with weaker literacy skills are given the opportunity to gain familiarity with the most difficult concepts and ideas, and are able to weave this understanding into their appreciation of new topics to ensure the learning is even further embedded.

Retaining key knowledge over time

Hermann Ebbinghaus discovered the 'forgetting curve' more than a century ago,[16] yet it is surprising how little my own teacher training and that of my

15. Ashford, K. (2020) 'Knowledge organisers: proceed with caution' in Birbalsingh, K (ed). *Michaela: the power of culture*, John Catt
16. Ebbinghaus, H. (1885) *Memory: a contribution to experimental psychology*

counterparts focused on the idea that we might need to cover topics more than once in order to ensure retention of key concepts. Of course, we have 'revision' time in the run-up to exams in Year 11, but how often do students begin the 'revision' of a topic as if they are learning it for the first time, particularly those who have weaker literacy skills, poor motivation or both?

Projected forgetting curve

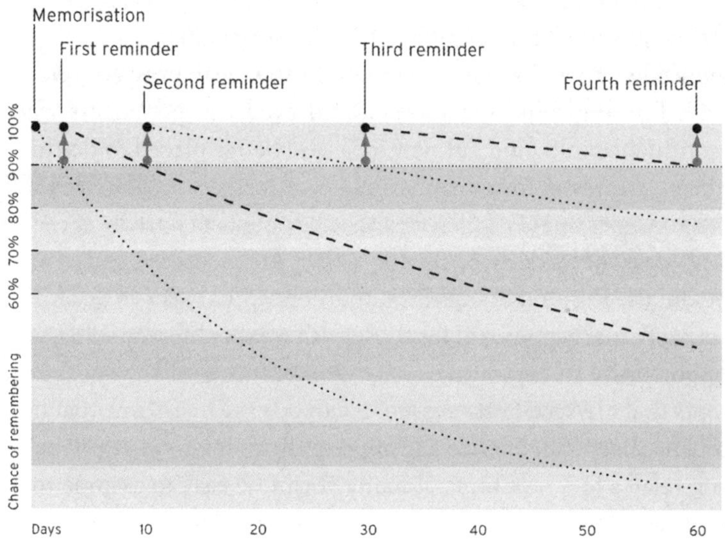

There are two key components to consider when seeking to ensure that students retain core knowledge over a number of years: retrieval strength and storage strength. Although they were not the first psychologists to make this distinction, Robert and Elizabeth Bjork set out to demonstrate the detrimental impact of simply focusing on short-term retrieval strength[17] – for example, teaching a unit of work, testing students at the end of it and considering the results a valid indicator of longer term learning. It is just as important to regularly circle back to key knowledge across the five years of a secondary school career and, most powerfully, at times when past knowledge can be connected to current learning to allow new connections to be made.

17. Bjork, EL and Bjork, RA (eds). (1996) *Memory*, Academic Press

When teaching Shelley's poem *Ozymandias* for the first time, a teacher is likely to teach the concept of 'hubris' in order to allow students to reflect on the arrogant folly of the central character. If students have already studied *Macbeth*, *A Christmas Carol* and *An Inspector Calls*, they can neatly apply the concept to central characters within each. This will not only support the long-term storage of the prior learning regarding these characters, but also provide a firm foundation for applying the concept of hubris to a new context.

Alongside this regular circling back within class, and the use of starter retrieval practice activities, it is important to maximise the benefits of home learning and the use of knowledge organisers to counteract the forgetting curve. At my school, Torquay Academy in Devon, one of our lead practitioners, Alex White, devised a method by which our knowledge organiser practice could ensure that past knowledge was systematically revisited. This shows how it looks in practice:

Week 1	Week 2	Week 3	Week 4	Week 5	Week 6	Week 7	Week 8
Week 1 content	Week 2 content	Week 3 content	Week 4 content	Week 5 content	Week 6 content	Week 7 content	Week 7 recap 1
Week 1 point 1	Week 2 point 1	Week 3 point 1	Week 4 point 1	Week 5 point 1	Week 6 point 1	Week 7 point 1	Week 7 recap 2
Week 1 point 1	Week 2 point 1	Week 3 point 1	Week 4 point 1	Week 5 point 1	Week 6 point 1	Week 7 point 1	Week 6 recap 1
Week 1 point 2	Week 2 point 2	Week 3 point 2	Week 4 point 2	Week 5 point 2	Week 6 point 2	Week 7 point 2	Week 6 recap 2
Week 1 point 2	Week 2 point 2	Week 3 point 2	Week 4 point 2	Week 5 point 2	Week 6 technique	Week 7 technique	Week 5 recap
Week 1 technique	Week 2 technique	Week 3 technique	Week 4 technique	Week 5 technique	Week 5 recap	Week 6 recap	Week 4 recap
Previous cycle W7	Week 1 recap 1	Week 2 recap 1	Week 3 recap 1	Week 4 recap	Week 4 recap	Week 5 recap	Week 3 recap
Previous cycle W7	Week 1 recap 2	Week 2 recap 2	Week 3 recap 2	Week 3 recap	Week 3 recap	Week 4 recap	Week 2 recap
Previous cycle W6	Previous cycle W7	Week 1 recap 1	Week 2 recap	Week 2 recap	Week 2 recap	Week 3 recap	Week 1 recap 1
Previous cycle W5	Previous cycle W6	Previous cycle W7	Week 1 recap	Week 1 recap	Week 1 recap	Week 2 recap	Week 1 recap 2

It was, of course, mind-boggling for students to attempt to flick from one knowledge organiser to another and back again, so we have developed our own bespoke homework books; these set out daily questions for students to answer that link to each of their knowledge organisers. This was a huge undertaking and it has taken several years to get to this point. However, it is a task that could be carried out by a non-teacher, so a worthy investment could be made in employing an administrator to create these books once the knowledge organisers are in place.

Alongside knowledge organisers and homework books, it can be useful to use online programmes such as Google Forms or Tassomai to allow students to self-test their knowledge and receive immediate feedback. Programmes such as Tassomai can 'learn' the concepts that a child finds particularly challenging to remember and present questions on those concepts more frequently. This can be especially useful for subjects such as science, which have an expansive knowledge base. In maths, online programmes such as Sparx give students the chance to revisit key knowledge, put it into practice immediately and gain feedback on their responses.

Barriers to developing a secure knowledge base

Curriculum development in schools has come a long way in recent years, so for most schools the development of knowledge organisers would not be too onerous. One temptation is to find existing knowledge organisers for your subject online and use those. It is very possible that this may work effectively, but the danger is that the knowledge does not match up precisely with what is taught. In my school, a central frustration for many students when we first introduced knowledge organisers was that what they were learning at home did not match up to what they were learning in class, and sometimes with the tests they sat at the end of the unit. This just can't happen. So, by all means look to the hundreds of existing knowledge organisers, but remember that the knowledge within them must be carefully sequenced and aligned with what is taking place in lessons.

There is also a large risk that the more powerful and useful homework becomes in enabling students to become experts in your subject, the further behind those who cannot or will not engage with homework will fall. It is vital that those students are identified early and supported to ensure their participation. This might mean they are enrolled in an after-school club where they can access support, so their school day simply ends later. This will be appropriate for some but not for the most disengaged. For those students, there must be a careful balance between the punitive detention as a consequence and the immediate follow-up to ensure the detention time is used effectively.

If students receive time within their school day for literacy support, a powerful use of this time would be to make sure homework is completed. The most effective literacy support enables students to access the literacy instruction they receive within their entire curriculum complement. Recapping key concepts and looking ahead to those that are coming up provide an excellent confidence boost and improve engagement with lessons that students feel they can be successful in.

Moving from PowerPoint displays to booklets

PowerPoint has certainly served a useful purpose within education, saving many hours of time that would have been spent writing up lesson plans, schemes of work and resources that then need to be brought to life using a whiteboard and pen. I don't think lessons are necessarily any 'better' than they were before as a result of using PowerPoint, but it has facilitated a shift towards shared curriculum planning, which has saved teachers many hours of duplication across departments.

This shared planning, along with PowerPoint itself, has been both a blessing and a curse. When done well, centralised resources are an excellent starting point: teachers can consider their own classes and adapt the resources to suit their context. Teachers will familiarise themselves with the lesson content and make sure they are clear what the teacher who produced the resource was 'getting at'; ideally, the overarching aims of a unit of work will be very clear, the knowledge and skills will be set out within the curriculum plans, and it will be obvious how this lesson ties in with those overarching aims. When done badly, however, a teacher who is juggling a challenging workload may only briefly look through a resource before the lesson. And, if the curriculum plan lacks coherence or the teacher has not received adequate CPD to get to grips with it, the students will experience a lesson that, at best, lacks coherence and, at worst, creates misconceptions that it will take some time to 'undo'.

Booklets and workbooks have existed in the classroom since more large-scale photocopying has become possible. Recently, more teachers are discovering the advantages of collating all the resources needed for a unit of work and presenting them either in a complete book of resources, or in a workbook that provides space for activities to be completed. A move from PowerPoint towards booklets/workbooks will not resolve issues that arise from an incoherent curriculum, and it is important that any shared curriculum resources are introduced alongside a solid foundation of subject-specific CPD (further discussed in chapter 15). This CPD time should include space for teachers to consider how best to adapt the resources for their classes, particularly those students who are furthest behind, and how to draw them into the modelling and questioning elements of the lesson. Students with lower literacy skills will particularly benefit from a teacher who has considered the moments of highest leverage within the lesson – those moments when they can be brought into the discussion and their understanding confirmed or established.

Centrally produced booklets not only improve the efficiency of delivering the curriculum, but they also provide students with the opportunity to look back over their learning and quickly refer to past lessons. This will prompt them in their understanding of new concepts and ideas, which will invariably link to a concept or idea they have encountered before. A child with poor literacy skills who uses a blank exercise book interspersed with worksheets is unlikely to find their own work a useful resource to revisit. If we consider a number of literacy issues that surround weaker literacy, we can see how this pattern develops:

- Illegible handwriting.
- Lack of motivation.
- Incomplete tasks.
- Low attendance.
- Lack of organisation.
- Weaker motor skills.

Just one of these traits is likely to result in a resource that, at best, has gaps and, at worst, is a tatty mess that the teacher hides at the bottom of the pile in a book scrutiny. A pre-printed booklet containing all the key content is far more likely to be treated with pride and respect by a child who appreciates the access it gives them to knowledge they may have missed when they were away. It also removes the painstaking trial of copying from the board, which can become a feature for the hurried but misguided science teacher keen to ensure that the most knowledge possible is covered as quickly as possible.

Booklets, particularly when used effectively alongside visualisers, are one of the few teaching methodologies that can begin to roll back the cumulative disadvantage phenomenon. So much of what we change within education to make it better often disproportionately benefits those who are already engaged and making excellent progress, but booklets offer a small window of opportunity to level the playing field for those who are falling behind. In a blog post,[18] Rosalind Walker writes incredibly persuasively about the use of booklets to facilitate Rosenshine's principles of instruction. She sums up the most striking argument for a move away from PowerPoint towards booklets:

> *'How much time in a typical week do students spend reading academic text? If you use booklets you are likely adding hours to this figure, which for many children would otherwise probably be zero. You can bring them into the world of reading for knowledge – just like that. What greater gift is there? And as we know, once phonics has been mastered, the amount and quality of text that is regularly read is the single most important factor in developing a child's reading ability – and we have the power to make this a reality, just through choosing this model.'*

18. Walker, R. (2020) 'Booklets, Rosenshine, Teach Like a Champion, and knowledge-rich curriculum'. Retrieved from: https://rosalindwalker.wordpress.com/2020/05/17/booklets-rosenshine-teach-like-a-champion-and-knowledge-rich-curriculum (accessed 19.09.20)

Booklets offer an opportunity to tighten up the strands of the reading rope. It becomes much easier to incorporate chunks of text and extracts into our lesson plans when we know we are not going to have to fight at the photocopier to get those extracts printed before the lesson. Incorporating extracts into PowerPoint is also problematic for those with weaker literacy skills, who can struggle to read extended pieces from the board.

From a behavioural perspective, it is particularly powerful to move away from the visual stimulus of PowerPoint towards booklets. I have taught a great number of classes with weaker literacy skills over the past 15 years, and it is fair to say that these classes often come with a share of characters who can cause disruption to the lesson. When I moved over to booklets, I realised that much of the distraction when they entered the room stemmed from their looking up at the board and then inevitably around to their friends. Booklets gave them their own independent learning space that allowed them to immediately get on without looking around. I believe that, given the right conditions, all students really do want to achieve success, and the booklets removed a large part of the distraction they faced when first entering the room.

The importance of routines and academic success to behaviour cannot be underestimated. Much of what I intend to outline in this book concerns how to set up environments where success is inevitable, even for those furthest behind.

The power of direct and explicit instruction

There has been a significant movement towards direct instruction in recent years and a wide range of accessible reading material is now available on this topic. In putting together this section, I am indebted to Adam Boxer for *The researchED Guide to Explicit and Direct Instruction*,[19] which he edited. I have condensed what I have learned from this guide and other sources, and attempted to express the centrality of direct instruction to developing literacy skills for those furthest behind.

19. Boxer, A (ed). (2019) *The researchED Guide to Explicit and Direct Instruction*, John Catt

Boxer describes Engelmann's programme of Direct Instruction as occupying an 'anti-Goldilocks zone of being the least known strategy with a frustratingly large impact'. The evidence provided by Project Follow Through[20] and substantiated by cognitive scientists such as Daniel Willingham demonstrates what many teachers instinctively believe to be true: that children make the most progress when the teacher is fully in control of the learning process and empowered to explicitly deliver content that students then practise with appropriate scaffolding and guidance.

It is important to appreciate Engelmann as the forerunner to Direct Instruction (with the capital letters) owing to the focus that Engelmann placed on the curriculum. As I have outlined, developing a secure knowledge base is fundamental to effective teaching and particularly fundamental for those with weaker literacy skills, who need explicit teaching of the background knowledge required to access the texts they will encounter across the curriculum. Rosenshine went on to develop Engelmann's approach, but with a sharp focus on the pedagogical aspects. Rosenshine's ideas have begun to receive greater attention – Tom Sherrington and Oliver Caviglioli's easily digestible guide *Teaching Walkthrus* breaks down the key elements.[21] However, as with everything I have outlined so far in this book, the curriculum must come first or students will continue to be disadvantaged, because although they will be learning more effectively, they will still be left with gaps that those with weaker literacy skills will struggle with the most.

It is my intention here to briefly outline Rosenshine's principles of instruction, and then explain how I have worked at my school with vice-principal Harrison Littler and lead practitioner Natalie Jones to make these elements a fundamental part of our 'blueprint' for teaching and learning. This is supported by our coaching process (further discussed in chapter 15). Essentially, rather than formalised lesson observations, for the past five years we have evolved our incremental coaching process, which involves each teacher receiving detailed feedback on one aspect of their

20. Meyer, LA, Gersten, RM and Gutkin, J. (1983) 'Direct instruction: a Project Follow Through success story in an inner-city school', *The Elementary School Journal*, 84:2, pp.241-252
21. Sherrington, T and Caviglioli, O. (2020) *Teaching Walkthrus,* John Catt

teaching after a short drop-in session each week. Rosenshine's principles of instruction, supported by Doug Lemov's *Teach Like a Champion* strategies,[22] provide a common framework and language that allow sharp focus on those small steps each teacher can make to improve their teaching and learning. This sits beside an ongoing departmental review of curriculum planning and strategies to personalise our teaching for those who need the most support. We have also been strongly influenced by the principles of teaching for mastery, further discussed later in this chapter.

Rosenshine's principles of instruction

1. Daily review.
2. Present new material using small steps.
3. Ask questions.
4. Provide models.
5. Guide student practice.
6. Check for student understanding.
7. Obtain a high success rate.
8. Provide scaffolds for difficult tasks.
9. Independent practice.
10. Weekly and monthly review.[23]

It is not difficult to see how such a wealth of research evidence supporting these principles has evolved, and how they provide a framework for success for all learners that disproportionately benefits students with weaker literacy skills. My school has created small action steps for coaches to work on with teachers in order to improve their practice, which you can see on the following pages. These have been taken from a wider 'playbook', a bespoke set of action steps relating to our 'principles of teaching'.

22. Lemov, D. (2015) *Teach Like a Champion 2.0*, Jossey-Bass
23. Rosenshine, B. (2010) *Principles of Instruction,* International Academy of Education. Retrieved from: www.orientation94.org/uploaded/MakalatPdf/Manchurat/EdPractices_21.pdf (accessed 19.09.20)

Principles of teaching

Teacher

Students

1 Retrieval practice: do now

Teacher

1. Write retrieval practice questions derived from a well-structured, sequenced curriculum that is centred around the core knowledge required to be successful within their subject.
2. Use a range of questions based around the curve of forgetting, deployed so that students are recapping new knowledge for the current cycle, and previously taught knowledge from earlier cycles and years.
3. Set expectations for a silent start to lessons, with 'do now' retrieval practice routinely the first activity.
4. Ensure 'right is right' responses are elicited from students during whole-class feedback.
5. Encourage students to reflect on areas of strength in their knowledge and what they need to focus on.

Students

1. Enter the room in a calm and orderly way and get started straight away without instruction.
2. Attempt all questions, giving an appropriate level of detail.
3. Aim to answer questions from memory, but use other sources of information if needed, such as exercise books or the TA Dictionary.
4. Be ready to give appropriately detailed verbal answers if called upon during feedback.
5. Record any corrections to responses in purple pen during class feedback.

2 Hear from an expert: teacher exposition

Teacher

1. Present new material in small steps.
2. Make connections with prior learning.
3. Pre-empt common misconceptions and tackle them explicitly.
4. Use cold calling and circulation to check for understanding.
5. Use 'no opt out' to ensure students are referring back to previously taught content and know where to find the answers.
6. Model the reading process where new information is given through extended written pieces. Use 'control the game' where appropriate.
7. Explicitly pre-teach key vocabulary needed to access new material.

Students

1. Give 100% of attention to the new content, making notes and completing activities.
2. Track the speaker.
3. Prepared to respond to cold calls, attempting an answer or referring to notes if unsure.
4. Use 'control the game' when reading extended writing pieces, being prepared to read aloud if called upon.
5. Attempt to use new and unfamiliar vocabulary verbally if called upon or within 'turn and talk'.

3 Modelling and deliberate practice: I do, we do, you do

Teacher

1. Have a clear idea of what 'right is right' looks like in their subject at the top grades.
2. Repeatedly model the underlying principles of what 'right is right' looks like through writing stems, vocabulary, problem-solving or practical aspects.
3. Model the steps to success, verbalising the cognitive processes and providing scaffolds.
4. Involve students in constructing excellent work through cold calling and inviting ideas from the class.
5. Gradually increase level of independent practice, with substantial time given for silent individual work. For most subjects this will involve at least some element of extended writing.

Students

1. Aspire to the highest levels of success and understand it will take hard work to achieve this.
2. Fully engage with practice, looking back over previous work or asking for support if unsure.
3. Take down model notes, answers or annotations that are shared.
4. Be prepared to give appropriately detailed ideas when cold called or raise hands to contribute to shared modelling process.
5. Have the perseverance and resilience to aim to achieve the highest levels within independent practice.

4 Progress check: demonstrate knowledge and skills

Teacher

1. Ensure ample opportunity for students to independently demonstrate what they have learned.
2. Circulate and engage proactively with the work students are producing.
3. Cold call students, using wait time appropriately to maintain accountability and judge progress.
4. Pay particular attention to Closing the Gap students and the progress they have made.
5. Ensure there is no opt out for students during the feedback process.
6. Remind students that format matters by insisting on full sentences, academic vocabulary and economy of language.
7. Show-call examples of student work.

Students

1. Use this time in a lesson to show off what they can do.
2. Ask for clarification and support from the teacher when needed.
3. Be prepared to respond when cold called.
4. Understand that 'I don't know' will not be accepted as an answer and be ready to engage in a discussion to arrive at the right answer.
5. Ensure that answers are in full sentences, use academic vocabulary and are concise.
6. Learn from the work of other students that is being shared.

Show call and modelling
What makes show call and modelling effective?

Try it out:

Action step	Key questions	Practice
Explicitly share the components of an effective response.	What are the components of an effective response? How might you make this explicit to students? How can you activate/introduce this knowledge during the teacher exposition? How can you make this information readily available for students to refer back to?	Prepare to model a response to a task. Script and practise the explicit sharing of the components that make for an effective response.
Make reference to success criteria.	Is there a clearly defined success criteria? Is it readily available for students to refer back to? If using an assessment criteria, is it clear how the highest marks are awarded, and the distinction between assessment bands made explicit?	Prepare to model a response to a task. Script and practise your explicit reference to success criteria in the process.
Narrate the thinking and steps required to produce an effective response.	Have you clearly modelled the steps that are needed to articulate the key knowledge in a way that achieves the highest marks? Have you provided scaffolds and prompts that are appropriate to the literacy levels of the students? Have you narrated your thinking, talking through any decision-making processes, and clearly articulated your thoughts at each stage of the modelling process?	Prepare to model a response to a task. Script and practise your use of 'narrate the thinking' to explicitly share your thought process and the steps involved.

Scaffolding and frameworks

Using precisely the right scaffold when it is most needed, then gradually withdrawing that scaffold at the right time, is particularly important for those with weaker literacy skills. Lev Vygotsky devised a theory of learning that will be familiar to most educators, as it cuts across the progressive/traditional lines of debate.[24] Educators can agree that there are things that children, particularly younger children, can learn on their own, and that as the level of challenge increases, the role of support also increases. Where disagreement arrives is in precisely how much support the 'master' of a topic should provide to an 'apprentice'. Should they provide clues and materials that students navigate alongside their peers while the teacher acts as a facilitator, or should they play a more direct role in the instruction of this new topic and provide scaffolds to enable students to achieve success? The following diagram illustrates the concept of the zone of proximal development in terms of scaffolding.

24. Vygotsky, LS. (1932) *Thought and Language*

Zone of proximal development (ZPD) and scaffolding

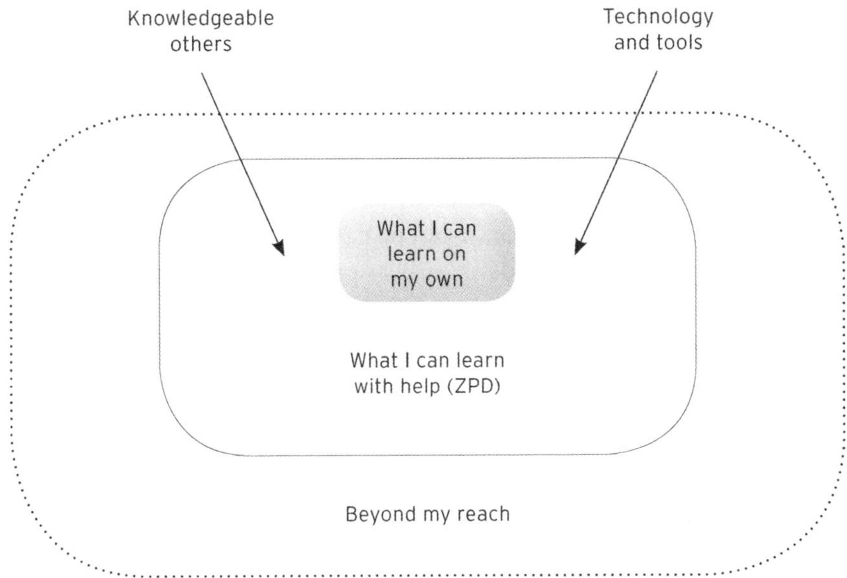

Adapted from source: Steve Wheeler, University of Plymouth, 2013

In direct and explicit instruction, the level of scaffolding required in order for a child, particularly one with weaker literacy skills, to be successful can be extensive and easy to underestimate.

Scaffolding was not a term ever used by Vygotsky, who instead referred more generally to the role of educators in supporting learners and their development. The term took on negative connotations throughout the coursework era of assessment, when different teachers had different interpretations of what was acceptable in terms of the scaffolding students received in order to complete a piece of coursework. But exam boards were always very clear: students must produce their own work. Attempts to resolve this were made with the introduction of controlled assessment, but this just resulted in more creative ways to provide scaffolds. It never really achieved what the assessment was designed for: to allow young people to become independent writers. A high-stakes accountability system combined with a key stage 3 that did not always tackle key literacy issues resulted in the exact reverse of this in many cases.

So now we have, in many instances, an examination-only system. Although the system was at first described as bad news for those with weaker literacy skills, particularly with the removal of the foundation paper for many subjects, instead what we have is the reverse: the ceiling has been removed for these students and the impetus is now on schools to ensure that independent literacy skills are foregrounded. With this strong focus on independence, it can be easy to believe that the kindest thing to do is remove scaffolds as early as possible – to get children used to writing 'on their own'. However, while it is important to build towards independence, it is even more important for success to be modelled and for those who will struggle most to be guided towards it gradually. The term 'extreme modelling' has been coined by Lyndsey Caldwell to refer to sentence stem scaffolds. Rebecca Lee presents some sentence stem sheets on her blog, which allow students to write analytically about challenging conceptual ideas from Year 7 onwards.[25] The aim is not to disenfranchise young people from their independence, but rather to facilitate their ability to emulate success in a way that feels safe. Young people must have the opportunity to experience success – to feel themselves writing in a way that emulates the very best as often as possible; the support must only be reduced when they are confident and able to do so.

Sentence starters, word banks and writing frames are vital tools for any teacher, but they are particularly important for students with weaker literacy skills. The key mistake that many teachers make is in their expectations of the outcome in providing the scaffold: just because a child is targeted a grade 4, that does not mean they need scaffolding to get to a grade 4. Give all children the scaffolding to reach a grade 9 and aim to ensure that this is practised frequently. A curriculum should build in the level of scaffolding that children receive at each stage, and even the most able will need significant scaffolding when they initially begin to write about a topic.

25. Lee, R. (2020) 'On sentence stems and "extreme modelling"'. Retrieved from: https://thelearningprofession.com/2020/08/04/on-sentence-stems-and-extreme-modelling (accessed 19.09.20)

It is important that there is flexibility within the scaffolding to ensure students have an element of choice and independence within their responses. And as their confidence increases, it is not so much a case of removing scaffolding, rather increasing the level of choice and complexity within it. For example, a child could be given a number of different phrases to choose from when introducing evidence, or when building upon or extending an idea. This exposure to academic language in context is key to developing confidence and writing stamina.

Oral scaffolding within teacher exposition is also often under-utilised and under-considered, with 'too much teacher talk' referred to as a trademark of poor teaching. In a blog post, Dawn Cox refers to a teacher's voice as 'the best differentiation tool they have'; she argues that a teacher can pitch their language appropriately for the group as they build up the schema of knowledge and repeatedly circle over more challenging concepts.[26] This connects to the central importance of dialogue and oral discussion for those students with the weakest literacy skills, and to how powerful it can be to particularly target them with questions framed in a way that ensure success before they put pen to paper. It also relates to the importance of subject-specific CPD sessions (discussed in chapter 15) where teachers have the opportunity to develop the quality and clarity of their expositions for challenging concepts, and particularly for ensuring that the students who are furthest behind are drawn into the follow-up discussion and checking for understanding.

Effective use of exemplars

One of the hardest things about taking on a new exam specification or teaching a new unit of work is the lack of available assessment materials and exemplars. But it can also be an exciting time, as one of the most useful things we can do when preparing to teach a unit is to place ourselves in the position of a student and attempt a paper ourselves. This

26. Cox, D. (2020) 'The best tool all teachers have for differentiation'. Retrieved from: https://missdcoxblog.wordpress.com/2020/01/14/the-best-tool-all-teachers-have-for-differentiation (accessed 19.09.20)

process is vital when planning out the curriculum, because although the key knowledge needed to be successful on a particular unit may have been meticulously planned, how to efficiently express that knowledge is not always straightforward – even for us as subject experts. Placing ourselves cognitively in the shoes of students is useful in determining the key academic language, phraseology and structure that are the components of a successful response. Going through this process allows us to consider the most appropriate scaffolding that will enable students to access this level of success.

The exemplars that we provide need to be very carefully selected, particularly those we give to students with weaker literacy skills. There must be a common thread that links the key content taught within lessons with the scaffolds that are provided during practice and any exemplars that are given. It is not that we cannot give a maximum mark essay to a student with weaker literacy skills; it is simply that this essay must be familiar in terms of its content, vocabulary, phraseology and structure. If all these elements have been explicitly taught, and are explicitly illustrated within the exemplar, a child with weaker literacy skills will begin to understand how they can reach this high ceiling.

It is worth noting that the use of exemplars can have the opposite effect to that intended if the above process is not followed. One of the most common misconceptions bred by a 'move to the next level' culture of assessment is that children learn best when given an example that is at the level above the one they are currently working at. In many subjects, it is, of course, entirely appropriate to ensure that students are only given tasks that correspond to the foundational knowledge they have established, and this is central to the mastery approach outlined by Mark McCourt in his book *Teaching for Mastery*.[27]

In subjects where extended written responses are required, I believe it can be very unhelpful to give a child who is 'currently attaining' a grade 3 a 'grade 4' piece of work (the inverted commas indicate that I am aware it is not possible to label a piece of work as inherently holding a grade

27. McCourt, M. (2019) *Teaching for Mastery*, John Catt

value). There are many reasons for this, not least because the 'grade 4' piece of work is likely to be difficult to follow grammatically, as it has been written by a student who struggles with their written expression. Ideas are likely to be confused and simplistic, and opportunities for misconceptions abound. The limitations that the student will place on their own attainment as a result of their teacher's perception of them are also a direct result of what is made explicit within the teaching materials. A child with weaker literacy skills will gain far more from a well-expressed top-mark example that has all the elements they are familiar with from prior explicit teaching.

A key difficulty with providing models and moving through the 'I do, we do, you do' Rosenshine methodology can be in ensuring that a student cannot just copy what has been written before and is able to independently apply the techniques they have seen used. When preparing for an extended piece of writing, before modelling the writing process it is also important to model the process of coming up with points to write about. When annotating source material within history, for example, the 'I do, we do, you do' process must be followed to generate a plan for, let's say, three paragraphs that will be written in response to the question. If practising writing, it is important that students do not stumble over the actual content that they will be referring to. Students with weaker literacy skills will struggle with the cognitive demands of generating original ideas and writing in a challenging new way at the same time. They must be well prepared with ideas before the writing begins. That is not to say that they should never have to attempt to generate ideas and responses, of course not, but it is important to single out each of these elements of practice and do one at a time, not both. It can be really powerful during questioning to challenge those students who struggle with literacy to orally express ideas, and to lead them towards expressing an idea that they can then go on to write about. There is nothing more rewarding than seeing students who so often orally express interesting and original thoughts in a position to begin writing them down.

A note on lesson length

I have worked in schools where lesson lengths have varied from 50 to 100 minutes and what feels like everything in between. The idea behind the 50-minute lesson was to keep students engaged and moving from one lesson to another at a fast pace – there were six lessons in a day, plus tutorial and four transitions. On a huge site, students would often end up with only 35 minutes of learning time if they had some distance to walk. Although understandable in a challenging context, this timetable was created based on a culture of low expectations – the expectation that children were unable to sit and focus for an hour. However, for those children with weaker literacy skills, these short lessons posed their own challenges: with six lessons of content to digest, moving quickly from one topic to another and then being expected to pick up the previous lesson's learning caused their heads to spin. It was unsurprising that they struggled to retain information.

Longer lessons offer adequate time for retrieval practice, introducing new content, modelling and practice. How often is the content and practice spread over two lessons, with days in between that cause learning to be forgotten? A lesson that lasts for longer than an hour offers students the opportunity to build a strong foundation of knowledge that can then be used as a secure basis for more challenging practice tasks. And for those classes that need it, a larger number of practice elements can be broken down into smaller chunks. Since moving to 100-minute lessons, I have been surprised by how efficiently content can be covered and the level of understanding that can be reached by the end. For example, when teaching poetry, it might usually take two lessons to teach the historical context and key vocabulary, then annotate the poem and write an analytical paragraph. But this entire sequence can be completed in one 100-minute lesson, without the need to recap in between.

So, when planning the timetable with behaviour and students with weaker literacy skills in mind, remember that it is not helpful for them to move from one short lesson to another. It is far more productive to ensure that longer lessons are appropriately chunked to offer a range of tasks that build to a higher collective understanding.

Part II

Creating classrooms where disadvantaged learners thrive: best practice within the subject disciplines

Chapter 2. English literature

A note on the development of the national picture

It has been an absolute pleasure to chart the movement of English literature to the core of the English curriculum since the start of my career in 2006. Back then, although literature was a component of the overall English GCSE, it was mainly assessed via coursework, and the drive towards a C grade meant students had incredibly varied experiences of the texts they were taught. In the worst cases, they essentially wrote up pre-prepared plans of small sections of texts, with very little exploration of themes beyond those that were part of the coursework question. The actual English literature GCSE was reserved only for those deemed worthy of such study – those who could afford to have time squeezed out of their English lessons to study a wider variety of texts in a much broader sense.

We went from this to an even more clearly defined bilateral system, in which some students studied both English literature and English language, and others studied for an 'English only' GCSE. The latter qualification was designed for weaker students but, in many exam boards, it was actually harder to pass than the English language GCSE. So, after the results debacle of 2012, we ended up with a huge number of students being entered for both qualifications but (again, in the worst cases) only actually studying for one. This turmoil placed heads of departments and KS4 coordinators under far greater pressure: it became increasingly challenging to 'keep up' with the changes and the results simultaneously held higher stakes than ever before. Many schools only realised the flaw in the system once they were on the receiving end of a shocking set of results, compounded by the mess of early entries and the cap on C grades.

As a result, English literature suffered for several years: schools, under the pressure of accountability systems, prioritised English language as this single qualification became the 'magic C grade' GCSE – a quick-fix solution in a curriculum quagmire. Cohorts of students often studied for multiple versions of the same language GCSE, but were told to put their names on the exam paper for their literature GCSE and it didn't matter how well they did. Heartbreaking.

Now, with the equal weighting of literature and language within accountability tables, it feels as if a new era has dawned. Suddenly we can place texts – whole texts! – at the heart of the English curriculum and achieve great results at the same time. It genuinely feels to me like the very best time to be an English teacher – and a teacher of literature.

What is 'core knowledge' in a study of literature?

It is fair to say that the department I have worked in over the past five years achieves excellent results. I feel it is important to frame the advice that follows in the context of the outcomes that have been achieved, particularly by our low prior attainers. In all good conscience, I am able to say that what we have done has improved the life chances of these young people, owing to the passport their English qualification has provided them with. It has been a privilege to work alongside Jen Brimming and Jamie Engineer, who have revolutionised the way English literature has been taught in order to achieve these exceptional outcomes.

The work they have done has brought the study of English literature to life, for students and staff. Our A-level take-up has increased exponentially, with two classes running in Years 12 and 13 – and this in a school with demographics classed as among the most deprived in the county. Aside from results days, the biggest joy for me can be found within my own classroom: when a Year 10 student who has struggled with their ability to read and write confidently tells me that Macbeth has been 'emasculated' by Lady Macbeth, and that this 'subverts the natural order' within Jacobean society. But he doesn't just tell me: he manages to produce a paragraph of writing under exam conditions, using these exact terms and providing appropriate references as evidence. Such an achievement is the result of disciplinary literacy.

It is important to circle back through the core knowledge that students need in order to be successful in a subject, and this is no different in English. It sounds blindingly obvious and a science teacher would look at me as if I were mad for suggesting any different. However, the cumulative nature of English has resulted in many decent teachers believing it is skills-based and that the texts selected are irrelevant provided the appropriate skills are taught. It is so important to consider how much a literature text, as with any other work of art, draws on what has gone before it. How can a child really appreciate the biblical connotations of the prophet-like inspector in *An Inspector Calls* if they have not previously been explicitly taught about the core Christian beliefs that underpin his damning warning of 'fire and blood and anguish'? It is not enough for a child with weaker literacy skills to have a sequence of lessons around this when they are taught the play in KS4. It is also not enough to expect a squeezed RS teacher to be able to fully cover all the bible stories that form such a significant part of our cultural heritage. It is up to English teachers to make explicit links between biblical concepts introduced by RS teachers and the influence of these concepts within the literary world.

So, how do we pin down the 'key' or 'core' knowledge within an English curriculum that has an infinitely broad range of texts and possibilities? The obvious answer is always: look at the exam! What skills are students being assessed on? Teach them those skills in various iterations from Year 7! Everyone wins, surely? Well, actually, to narrow down the curriculum so drastically would result in a great number of losers, and I would argue that it is unlikely to achieve the best outcomes, either in terms of exam grades or in terms of passion for the subject. The texts that make up the end-of-KS4 exams are just a few of a huge number that could have been chosen. Some schools go so far as to teach exam texts in Year 9 and then again in Year 11 – does this really give students a rich and varied understanding of literature, particularly those students who read very little outside school?

Instead, we should ask: what critical, historical and cultural knowledge must a student possess in order to make an informed judgement about

Y7 - Cycle 1	Y7 - Cycle 2	Y7 - Cycle 3	Y7 - Cycle 4
Lord of the Flies (transition)	Middle ages and morality	*Romeo and Juliet* (central text and extracts)	The natural world (Romantic poetry)
Ass.: analysis of language in short extract from *Lord of the Flies*	Ass.: persuasive article on gender stereotyping	Ass.: extended analysis of Shakespeare's presentation of Lord Capulet	Ass.: comparison of *Ode to the West Wind* and one other poem
Skills focus: literature A01 - main ideas, finding evidence A02 - basic language analysis Focus on annotation and using TA paragraph structure	Skills focus: language Persuasive writing main focus/ also builds basic skills of non-fiction analysis Supplemented by non-fiction from a range of authors	Skills focus: literature A01 - main ideas, finding evidence A02 - deeper language analysis A03 - context and writer's intentions	Skills focus: literature A01 - high-level points, finding evidence A02 - deep language analysis A03 - context and writer's intentions
Critical content focus: society, tyranny, democracy, morality, representation of race, British empire (extracts from a range of authors referred to)	Critical content focus: power of the Church, race and the 'three continents', gender stereotyping, patriarchy, class differences, authority	Critical content focus: tragic conventions (hamartia, peripeteia, tragic hero, etc.), patriarchy, monarchy, religion, hierarchy, masculinity, diversity within Elizabethan London	Critical content focus: Romantic poetry, Industrial Revolution, exploitation of working classes, power of nature, corruption, expansion of British empire and resistance to it

Y8 - Cycle 1	Y8 - Cycle 2	Y8 - Cycle 3	Y8 - Cycle 4
The Gothic	Dickens	War and conflict poetry	*Of Mice and Men*
Ass.: extended analysis of insanity in *The Yellow Wallpaper*	Ass.: extended analysis of Dickens' presentation of utilitarian education	Ass.: evaluative response, *Children in Wartime*	Ass.: extended analysis of Steinbeck's presentation of Curley's wife
Skills focus: literature A02 - language analysis A03 - applying context	Skills focus: literature and language A01 - high-level points, finding evidence A02 - language analysis A03 - applying context and writer's intentions One or two lessons a week working on writing skills	Skills focus: language P1 Q4 (evaluation) A01 - main ideas, finding evidence A02 - basic language analysis	Skills focus: literature A01 - high-level points, finding evidence A02 - deep language analysis A03 - context and writer's intentions
Critical content focus: dehumanisation, patriarchy, class differences, social anxieties, xenophobia, supernatural, the Black Gothic revival	Critical content focus: new Poor Law, industrialisation, class difference, Dickens on education, utilitarianism	Critical content focus: soldiers and identity, reality vs propaganda, effect of conflict on psyche	Critical content focus: marginalisation of social groups, social hierarchy, civil rights movement and emancipation

Y9 - Cycle 1	Y9 - Cycle 2	Y9 - Cycle 3	Y9 - Cycle 4
Animal Farm	Reading and writing prose	Viewpoint writing - poetry and non-fiction	Practical criticism
Ass.: extract analysis linking theme across text	Ass.: descriptive writing	Ass.: persuasive writing	Ass.: unseen extract analysis
Skills focus: literature A01 - high-level points, finding evidence A02 - deep language analysis A03 - context and writer's intentions	Skills focus: language Descriptive writing: motif, symbolism, setting, atmosphere, characterisation, analepsis, cyclical structure	Skills focus: language Persuasive writing main focus/ also builds skills of poetry and non-fiction analysis and comparison of perspectives	Skills focus: language Analysis of fiction and non-fiction with focus on writers' tools. Focus on gaining independence in connecting tools with ideas
Critical content focus: capitalism, exploitation, oppression, surplus-value, false consciousness, authoritarianism, parody	Critical content focus: writing as their own source of power - adopting writers' tools to communicate their own ideas and perspectives, drawing on previously covered content	Critical content focus: emancipation, discrimination, culture, institution, colonialism, commodification, nationalism, civil rights, freedom and democracy	Critical content focus (analysing writers' tools): drawing together of grammatical functions, figurative language, single word choice, discourse, language of class, gender and power

a text by the time they leave school? Which texts will combine to build this knowledge from the moment they arrive in Year 7 to the end of their statutory careers in Year 11? What will ignite a passion for literature that they will have for the rest of their lives?

At Torquay Academy, we took a historical approach to designing our key knowledge: rather than working backwards from the exam, we decided to start (as far as possible) at the beginning. We looked at all the most significant literary movements and organised the KS3 curriculum sequentially from this (see opposite). After an initial transition unit that introduces students to literature study and finding their own voices as writers, they work from Chaucer through to Shakespeare, the Romantics, the Gothic, the social justice of Dickens, and conflict poetry from the First World War through to the modern era. Each unit is supplemented with texts that pre-date this era and are essential to cultural literacy, such as Bible stories and Homer's *The Odyssey*.

Due to the predominance of 'dead white men' on the KS4 examination syllabus, there is a definite problem within many schools when it comes to ensuring that students have access to a wider range of voices and perspectives. Many have attempted to resolve this by placing a 'texts from other cultures' unit in their curriculums, which opens up further issues. Why should diverse voices be squeezed into this 'separate' category? Surely this perpetuates the 'othering' that is itself part of the problem?

Instead, it is incredibly important to weave and incorporate a range of voices into *every* unit we teach. For example, the whole 'golden era' of expansion and colonialism is central to an appreciation of any Shakespearean text, not just *The Tempest*. The language is rich in references that demonstrate how Elizabethan and Jacobean culture was greatly influenced by this period of global exploration; perceptions of this colonial empire shaped society. Shakespeare imagined that Caliban's speeches would echo those of the enslaved: 'You taught me thy language so I learnt how to curse'; 'This is my island'; the 'sounds and sweet airs' he uses to describe his homeland. But it is important to point out that Shakespeare is putting words into the mouths of the colonised, and to interrogate how he gained inspiration for these words.

An exploration of race during the Elizabethan and Jacobean eras would be fascinating and should be considered an element within a broader study of Shakespeare's work. It is also important to look beyond messages of subjugation and slavery within these contexts, and ensure that representation is ultimately empowering: Caliban and Ariel are both liberated at the end of *The Tempest*, which opens up the introduction of postcolonial literature. Just because students are in Years 7 or 8, that does not mean they are incapable of appreciating that we now live in a postcolonial era. We must lay the foundations for an appreciation of that.

The critical lens of postcolonial theory is a valuable one to equip students with, in any unit of work. We call our exercise books 'critic's journals', because part of becoming literate within the study of literature is learning to apply a variety of critical lenses to any text that is studied. This is part of building that complex web of 'velcro'[28] that allows students to make connections within and between texts, within and between literary eras, and within and between their own lives and experiences. Early on, students should be able to read a text and consider questions such as: how are women represented within this story? Who has written this text and why might they have represented women in this way? For example, Lady Macbeth is presented as a dangerous and subversive figure by Shakespeare as he builds up her power only to dramatically tear it down; his representation demonstrates what a Jacobean audience knew – that women can be powerful. But her fate demonstrates the dangers of this power and invites the audience to heed this warning. What might be a feminist reading of this text? This critical skill is vital in the study of all texts.

Developing students' critical abilities is key to opening up not just the study of a text at GCSE, but any text they encounter in their lives. As I will cover in chapter 11, on media studies, we live in an era where information is never in short supply, but the way that information is presented has never been more loaded.

28. Hirsch Jr, ED. (1996) *The Schools We Need and Why We Don't Have Them*, Doubleday

Breaking the ceiling

Essentially, everything I have discussed so far has been about building that foundational knowledge and teaching students to 'think like a literature critic'. But how can students be aided to commit their thoughts to the page in a way that does justice to the quality of the ideas that they so often express orally? The answer is simple: explicit modelling and practice, as we discussed in detail in chapter 1. This section will demonstrate how this practice can be structured in English literature, alongside teaching of the core knowledge required in order to write about the texts successfully.

Another corner of debate within the educational world has been the extent to which students should learn formulas and acronyms to facilitate their ability to remember to core 'ingredients' of literature study. And, as with so many of these debates, the false dichotomy is unhelpful. Yes, those students who mechanically move from an uninspiring point to a bolted-on quotation and follow up with a comment that essentially repeats their point are not going to be credited highly. I would argue that part of the problem here is not so much the formula but the student's lack of understanding, which prevents them from being able to produce an effective response. Put simply, they don't have that firm and secure knowledge. This leads them to become tied up in knots and use the frame as a crutch as opposed to a springboard.

Equally, there are students who have a great understanding of a text and write about it at length, but rarely provide any evidence and fail to closely examine the writer's deployment of techniques in order to communicate meaning. In most exam boards, examiner training for literature breaks down the assessment objectives into three key areas: the what, the how and the why. This has been written about extensively by Becky Wood[29] and adopted as a sensible and effective cornerstone of writing about texts in literature. The reason students with weaker literacy skills still struggle to reach the higher bands despite having a great oral comprehension of the text is that they simply lack the practice in analytical writing. Often, the students who need the most practice are challenged to write the least.

29. Wood, B. (2018) 'Why I no longer PEE'. Retrieved from: https://justateacherstandinginfrontofaclass.wordpress.com/2018/10/28/why-i-no-longer-pee (accessed 13.10.20)

I have worked in schools where, in the name of differentiation, 'top set' students are regularly given extended essay-writing practice while lower sets are only asked to write a paragraph. If any differentiation were to take place, it should be to reverse this trend. Those who most struggle to write need teachers who believe in their ability to get better. I have worked for many years with children who find writing difficult and it is incredible to see how they grow and develop, particularly when they have a secure knowledge base and are keen to show it off.

To support consistency in the journey from KS3 to KS4, and between a variety of teachers, we have found that it is useful for students to have an agreed structure that they can draw upon to support their analysis of literature. This is based upon David Didau's reading ladder, which takes students through the process of 'zooming in and out'.[30] The framework for this is on the opposite page, alongside an example that puts it into practice. Students are not constrained by this structure; rather, it offers a word bank of useful phrases. Our weakest students cling to it for dear life and it is not until they sit mock papers in Year 10 that we begin to remove this scaffold. By that point, they have internalised the processes that enable them to express their interpretation of a text. It is heartening to see the change in students who in the past might have referred to characters as real people: from 'Mr Birling is a selfish capitalist' to 'Priestley uses Mr Birling as a tool to highlight the narcissism of capitalist ideas'.

We find that more able students internalise the process of 'what, how, why' and begin to write lucidly across a whole text. Some students are so able that they arrive in Year 7 and only pay lip service to that structure when writing about *Lord of the Flies*, as they are so overwhelmed with the sheer number of references and connections they wish to make across the text, and they fly off in their own directions that are rooted in the core principles of literature study. Primary schools do a fantastic job of building children's confidence as writers and it is important to capitalise on that with those students who are already at the point where such structures can prove to be more of a hindrance.

30. Didau, D. (2011) 'Zooming in and out'. Retrieved from: https://learningspy.co.uk/english-gcse/zooming-in-and-out (accessed 20.11.20)

Exemplar paragraph

Dickens uses *A Christmas Carol* to show his readers the benefits of close, loving family life and this is shown clearly when Scrooge watches the Cratchit family on Christmas Day. Despite being 'not well dressed', Dickens describes the Cratchits as 'happy, grateful, pleased with one another, and contented with the time'. Here Dickens is using positive adjectives to create an impression of a model, happy family. This is emphasised by Dickens' use of listing, which almost sounds hyperbolic, perhaps highlighting that this happy vignette serves to juxtapose with Scrooge's isolation. Furthermore, the fact that Dickens has the family draw the 'deep red' curtains to 'shut out cold and darkness' is effective in that it demonstrates that the 'cold' and 'dark' of the harsh Victorian society can be forgotten if you have a loving family. The use of 'deep red' has connotations of love and togetherness, further highlighting the important intimacy of family life. Alternatively, the metaphor of the curtains could reinforce Dickens' message that the poor are not 'surplus' to requirements, as the shut curtains could symbolise Scrooge's blindness to the fact that there are real people behind the 'curtains' of poverty, people with families that love and care for them. In the Cratchits, Dickens constructs an ideal family for his readers, something Dickens, who had an absent father, did not experience. Perhaps Dickens uses the idealised Cratchit family in order to urge people to recognise that family is the key to happiness.

Point is conceptual and clearly linked to the question.

Explores how the evidence proves the point being made. Use of the writer's name shows awareness of the text as a conscious construct.

'Furthermore' adds a second embedded quotation to create a more convincing argument.

An **alternative interpretation** is offered. The analysis is conceptual and insightful. Subject terminology is well used.

Evidence is introduced clearly and evaluatively using a modal adverb. References are well chosen, short and embedded into a sentence.

Zooms in on a technique, exploring the effect on the audience using subject terminology.

The second piece of evidence is **insightfully analysed** with another **zoom**. Analysis is linked to context and writer's purpose.

The paragraph concludes by **zooming out** and linking to the writer's purpose and context.

Writing frame

The writer uses [build your point]...

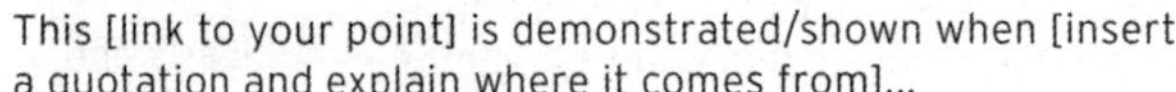

This [link to your point] is demonstrated/shown when [insert a quotation and explain where it comes from]...

This evidence/scene/description presents [simply explain quotation]... Ultimately, it reveals/shows/demonstrates [fully explain and link to point]...

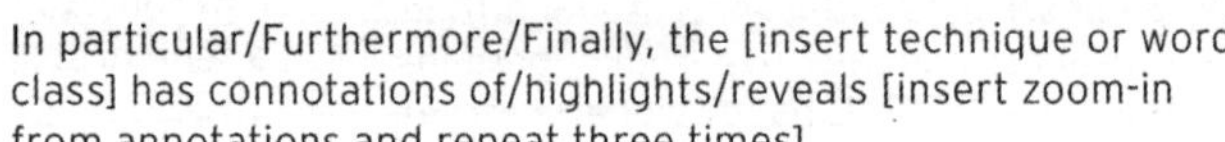

In particular/Furthermore/Finally, the [insert technique or word class] has connotations of/highlights/reveals [insert zoom-in from annotations and repeat three times]...

This argument/claim/thesis is further supported by [insert a second supporting quotation]... This articulates/demonstrates/reveals [explain and analyse supporting quotation]...

Perhaps the writer's intentions here are to/Perhaps the writer is trying to suggest [explain the writer's intentions clearly and link to context]...

Once students reach Year 11, they must regularly practise the application of their ideas and the scaffolds can be gradually left in the background as they gain the fluidity of their voices. At my school we cover all the literature content in Year 10, so Year 11 can effectively be divided into revision and practice of literature essays and the linked teaching of each element of the language paper. Our students write a whole essay every week, because they will achieve most highly when they have learned the key elements of a variety of potential questions, and when they become dexterous in their ability to apply similar analytical points to different questions. We have set up so many systems to allow the learning of key knowledge, but unless students can apply this knowledge regularly and consistently, then they will not have the ability to organise their thoughts in a way that demonstrates their potential in an exam situation.

Students must also build stamina in writing for sustained periods. We achieve this not by chucking all four papers at them in a fortnight every now and again, but by allowing them to spend solid chunks of 45 minutes just writing without notes. They are told the exam question in advance and part of their homework each week is to prepare their responses and learn them. The writing frame included opposite is always visible to them, but by the end of the year it is only the very weakest students who still rely on it. There are occasions within mocks when the scaffold is taken away, but a key part of revision is internalising those analytical phrases, so we want to keep them in the foreground for as long as possible.

I mentioned earlier that our students study *Lord of the Flies* in Year 7. This, to me, is a perfect choice for two reasons. Firstly, it offers the engagement and joy of literature: the opening few chapters allow students to meet the characters of Ralph and Piggy, and to immediately appreciate and recognise the dynamics within the relationship. We meet Ralph and Piggy in a moment of high drama and curiosity: an island without adults, exciting and terrifying in equal measure. Secondly, *Lord of the Flies* is actually much easier to write about than many books aimed at younger readers. The language is rich in symbolism, which spells out the key themes for even the weakest students. The attempt made by some of the boys to maintain law and order can be so easily juxtaposed with the desire of others to act out their more primal desires, descending further and further into 'savagery'. William Golding essentially packs every page with references to 'gold', 'sunlight', 'darkness', 'shadows'. I have read brilliant analytical responses from the weakest students because it practically teaches itself. There is also a great play script that can be used to supplement the teaching and further increase engagement.

It is particularly important to critique the way in which Golding represents the 'savagery'; the text offers an opportunity for students to develop their postcolonial critical lens. What attitudes towards race does Golding express throughout the novel as a whole? With any text, it is vital to pose these questions and invite children to consider the way in which the ideas of the time are represented and critiqued. Year 7 may be considered early to introduce children to such issues; I would argue that they have been introduced to them already within their daily lives. Tackling these issues head-on gives students an opportunity to place what they have read, heard about and experienced within a wider cultural framework, and this is infinitely preferable to pretending that the issues don't exist.

At Torquay Academy, we are proud that our students are so confident in the discipline of literature study. We are proud that many students who arrive with below average KS2 scores go on to achieve the grades they need to study English literature at A-level. Many might assume that extensive essay writing and a relentless focus on learning key conceptual knowledge would turn students off literature. We have found the exact reverse to be true. For many students, it has illuminated what has always been a darkened world. Previously, books have not 'been for them' for a whole range of reasons, but they leave us with the ability to appreciate how literature brings to life fundamental questions about their existence in the world.

Chapter 3. English language

The connection between language and literature

English language has only existed as a GCSE in its own right since 2012 (first entry). As discussed in the previous chapter, there has been much shift and change over the past two decades and I have been teaching just long enough to have delivered the original iteration of the 'English' GCSE. This GCSE had a wide remit: it involved speaking and listening modules, reading media texts, reading poetry, creative writing, persuasive writing, writing for an audience (for example, a film review) and literature in the form of coursework that analysed Shakespeare and a novel. As an NQT, I worked in a school that entered all students for media studies alongside English, and those in the top sets were also entered for English literature. My abiding memory of this experience is drafting and redrafting coursework – mountains of it.

It is interesting to look back and see how the qualification has evolved and the impact the different versions have had on students with weaker literacy skills. The argument for coursework has always been that it allows for these students to shine; that, given the additional time and space, those with weaker literacy skills can avoid being disadvantaged. The problem with this approach is that, paired with increasing accountability pressures, students with weaker literacy skills have ultimately been more disadvantaged in many schools – not because they did not gain their magical C grade in English, but because they did not *earn* that grade. The often heavily scaffolded coursework that accounted for 20% of the qualification, alongside the heavily 'massaged' speaking and listening scores that comprised another 20%, resulted in a generation of young people leaving school without the ability to read and write effectively, but with a certificate stating that they could. This was around the time that education became compulsory to 18, so although many teachers felt they were doing the right thing by giving young people this passport to higher level study, they were ultimately cheating their students out of the additional teaching that they needed in these vital skills.

In 2012, I was fortunate to discuss the aims behind what would become the English language GCSE with Tim Oates of Cambridge Assessment, when he taught a module of the master's degree I was studying for. Oates had been an adviser during the 2010 qualification reforms, which were to replace the qualifications that had only recently been introduced by the previous government, and I was interested in how he felt about the removal of literature from the 'English' GCSE. He persuasively explained that a key priority for the government was to ensure that young people were able to read and write, and that this in itself was worthy of a qualification. I later learned the details of the accountability system in which entry for literature ensured the double weighting for language; it was clear that literature was prioritised not just for the more able as an 'add-on', but as a body of knowledge that all children should have access to. It is difficult to look back now at the limitations that were previously placed on young people's achievements and on their access to a subject that is now so fundamental to our teaching.

A knowledge-based whole-school curriculum

As I argued in chapter 1, every discipline has a role to play in providing the essential background knowledge that a child needs in order to access the unseen texts they will encounter in their language exam – and any text they will encounter in their adult lives. When looking back through all the English language exam papers set by AQA since the new specifications in 2016, I found that geographical knowledge was often important in unlocking the central meaning in the unseen texts (see chapter 7 for a summary table). For example, in one text the main character is skiing in the Pyrenees and becomes involved in an avalanche. The narrative contains several clues that an avalanche is about to take place and students with a grounding in geographical knowledge would appreciate the danger in the distant rumbles that are described. Early on, the scene is described as calm and perfect – too perfect, an experienced reader would understand.

Students with weaker literacy skills would not pick up on these clues and would perhaps be nonplussed by the distant rumbling if they had never heard of an avalanche. However, with this geographical grounding, they would immediately recognise the mountainous setting as one of danger. The repeated references to snow would set off alarm bells if they understood what this snow could lead to; this, in turn, would lead them to spot other clues suggesting imminent danger.

One of the greatest misconceptions of literacy, in my view, is that it doesn't matter how you teach it or the texts you use. It is not true that the skills can be developed almost in isolation from everything else – that you can give a child a text about mountains and get them to infer the impending danger without first introducing them to the concept of an avalanche and how avalanches occur. As the Scarborough reading rope illustrates (page 18), background knowledge is key to comprehension, as is vocabulary knowledge. Any text given to students must be carefully considered in light of the pre-teaching required to access it. Of course, it is important for young people to have strategies for attempting to independently access unfamiliar vocabulary, and this is discussed in chapter 14, but we need to consider which skill we are developing in our lessons. Should every lesson be about seeking to overcome barriers in accessing background knowledge and vocabulary, or should some lessons be devoted to developing the skill of inference without having to additionally overcome the barrier of basic comprehension? I would argue that it is impossible to teach the skill of inference *without* basic comprehension. I have learned this through many years of attempting to draw out inferences and connotations from children who just do not have the background knowledge or cultural literacy skills to make the connections I am hoping for.

To give an example, I might teach a text in which a character ritualistically washes their hands, or a persuasive piece in which a writer refers to a politician 'washing their hands' of a matter. A child who has a firm grounding in religious studies would appreciate the connection between sin, guilt and becoming cleansed. A child without this grounding might be able to understand that the character/politician is associated with being dirty, and might then make the connection between feeling dirty and feeling guilty, but they will find it more difficult to make these connections and even harder to articulate these ideas without prompting. If we wish to develop a child's ability to infer, and to express their inferences in writing, we need to carefully pre-teach the ideas needed in order to fully access the text. To further the example above, a useful pre-teaching exercise would be to briefly tell the story of Pontius Pilate and how he 'washed his hands' of the plight of Jesus as a way of symbolically absolving himself of guilt. This could be supplemented by examples from literature, such as Lady Macbeth's declaration of 'Out, damned spot!' and the overall motif of water, cleansing and guilt within *Macbeth*.

It is, of course, impossible to prepare students for every eventuality within the unseen element of their language papers, but a five-year literature and language course, alongside a knowledge-rich cross-school curriculum, will give them a strong foundation of background knowledge and vocabulary that they can draw upon not just in these exams, but with any text they encounter in their adult lives.

The role of political understanding in argument writing

Reading and writing are inextricably linked, but are often taught in isolation. For example, we may plan a unit on persuasive speeches in which the main focus is analysis of existing speeches, and because the 'outcome' of this particular unit is a piece of analytical writing, writing analytical paragraphs becomes the driver of each lesson. This is completely logical and, cognitively, it does make sense to choose to focus on developing either reading or writing skills. However, what is less logical is to have a persuasive writing unit later in the course that does not connect back to this previous unit or give a great deal of exposure to examples of persuasive writing. I have taught many units that are defined as either 'reading' or 'writing', when it would make more sense to have slightly longer units that give children the opportunity to develop both of these skills.

It is not necessary to carry out formalised assessments of reading and writing that result in a grade that feeds into a reporting system. Writing, especially, can be something that is experimented with and enjoyed, particularly in KS3. Persuasive writing connects perfectly with oracy and offers children the chance to express how they feel about a particular topic. However, many of us will have been surprised by how disengaged young people can be from the political landscape and by how challenging it can be to encourage them to feel passionate about something. It is important to recognise that young people can lack confidence in articulating their thoughts on topics they do not feel knowledgeable about. This may seem strange: young people have unfettered access via social media to information about what is happening in the world, so how can they not form an opinion? But that volume of information can be overwhelming and confusing, and even more so for students with weaker literacy skills or from homes where conversations about politics either are particularly one-sided or do not take place at all. It is not surprising that many young people choose not to engage.

As educators, we have a responsibility to instil an appreciation of the key political debates that are current and relevant today, but also to offer the historical background to these political debates so that students can see how, particularly in recent years, politics has become so polarised. To appreciate the literature texts they encounter and the persuasive pieces within their language papers, young people need to understand, for example, what is meant by left wing and right wing. The graphic included overleaf, from David McCandless at Information is Beautiful,[31] provides an excellent overview of the differences between left and right; it would be useful to discuss these not only in English lessons, but also in history and other subjects in which students need to understand the basis of political decisions.

31. https://informationisbeautiful.net

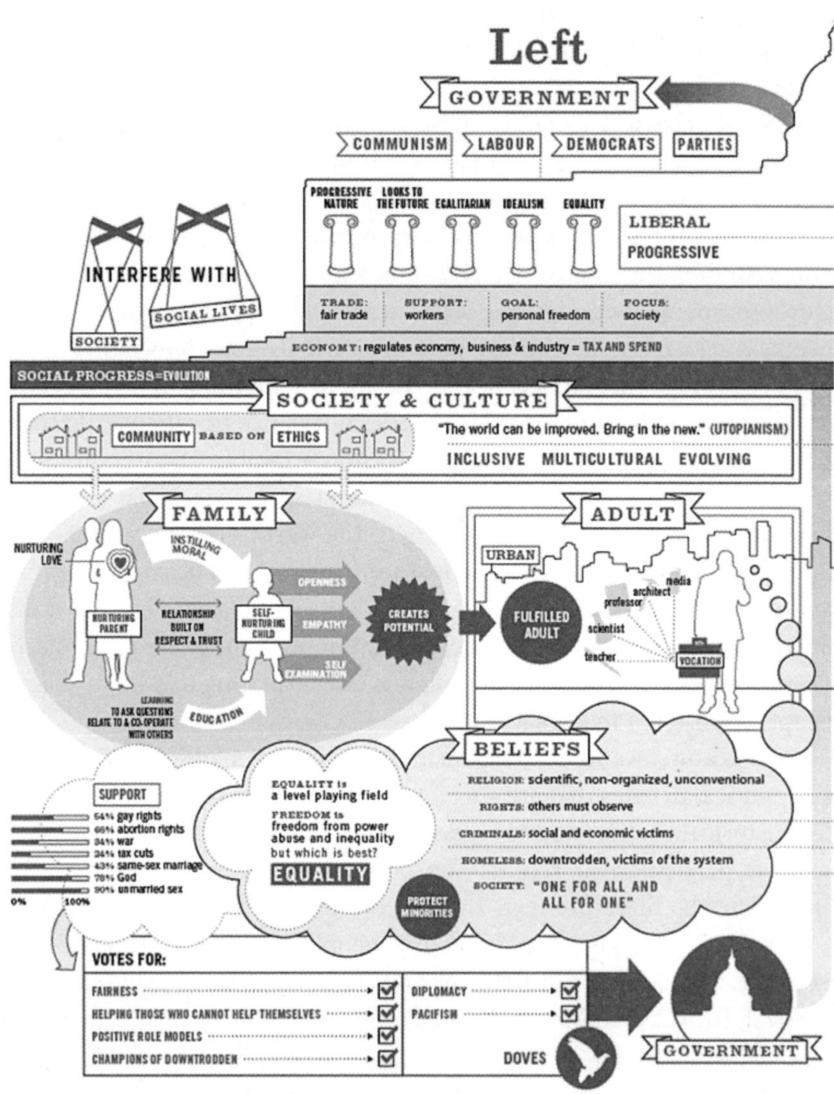

Source: David McCandless at InformationIsBeautiful.net

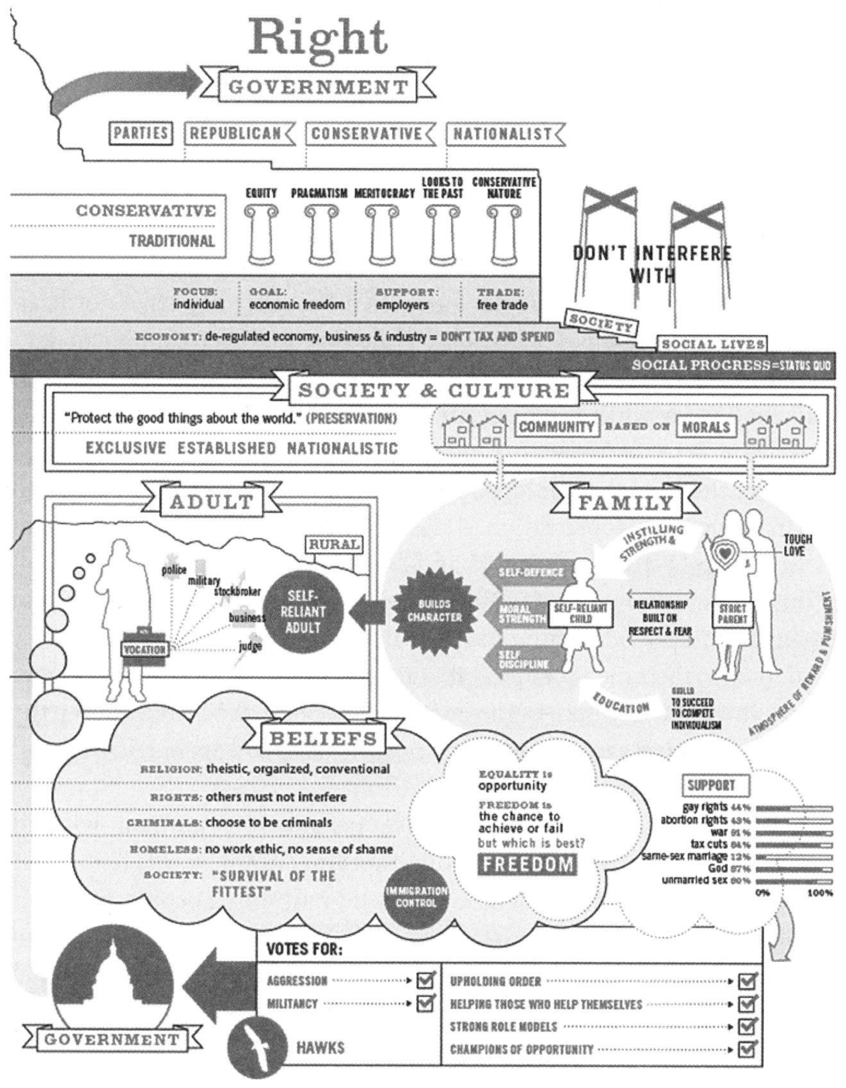
Right
GOVERNMENT
PARTIES
REPUBLICAN
CONSERVATIVE
NATIONALIST
CONSERVATIVE
TRADITIONAL
EQUITY
PRAGMATISM
MERITOCRACY
LOOKS TO THE PAST
CONSERVATIVE NATURE
FOCUS: individual
GOAL: economic freedom
SUPPORT: employers
TRADE: free trade
ECONOMY: de-regulated economy, business & industry = DON'T TAX AND SPEND
DON'T INTERFERE WITH
SOCIETY
SOCIAL LIVES
SOCIAL PROGRESS=STATUS QUO
SOCIETY & CULTURE
"Protect the good things about the world." (PRESERVATION)
EXCLUSIVE ESTABLISHED NATIONALISTIC
COMMUNITY BASED ON MORALS
ADULT
RURAL
police
military
stockbroker
business
judge
VOCATION
SELF-RELIANT ADULT
BUILDS CHARACTER
FAMILY
SELF-DEFENCE
MORAL STRENGTH
SELF-DISCIPLINE
SELF-RELIANT CHILD
INSTILLING STRENGTH &
RELATIONSHIP BUILT ON RESPECT & FEAR
STRICT PARENT
TOUGH LOVE
EDUCATION
SKILLS TO SUCCEED TO COMPETE INDIVIDUALISM
ATMOSPHERE OF REWARD & PUNISHMENT
BELIEFS
RELIGION: theistic, organized, conventional
RIGHTS: others must not interfere
CRIMINALS: choose to be criminals
HOMELESS: no work ethic, no sense of shame
SOCIETY: "SURVIVAL OF THE FITTEST"
IMMIGRATION CONTROL
EQUALITY is opportunity
FREEDOM is the chance to achieve or fail
but which is best?
FREEDOM
SUPPORT
gay rights 44%
abortion rights 43%
war 81%
tax cuts 84%
same-sex marriage 12%
God 87%
unmarried sex 80%
0%
100%
VOTES FOR:
AGGRESSION
MILITANCY
HAWKS
UPHOLDING ORDER
HELPING THOSE WHO HELP THEMSELVES
STRONG ROLE MODELS
CHAMPIONS OF OPPORTUNITY
GOVERNMENT

In persuasive/argument writing, young people do not have to assume a position that they believe themselves. This is powerful for them to understand, as often it can be more straightforward to argue from the point of view of an imagined person, rather expressing their own (possibly more sensible and balanced) opinions. We need to prepare young people to be able not only to argue for what they believe in and to fight their own corner, but also to place themselves in the position of those whose political opinions differ from their own. This is a vital life skill that many adults struggle with, often because they have not been taught the fundamental principles that, for example, capitalism and socialism are based upon.

It can be easy when teaching *An Inspector Calls,* for example, to focus entirely on Priestley's socialist message and reinforce the caricatures he creates of the capitalist middle class. It is important, however, to ground this message in an appreciation of how we arrived at the capitalist system we live in today and the benefits and freedoms afforded to us as a result of this system. We must navigate this complex political landscape without prejudice and provide young people with the balanced information they need to form their own opinions about politics. Those children who score highly in persuasive writing tasks do so because they understand the arguments both for and against the position they are arguing from, and are able to counterbalance these effectively.

It is possible to write an effective persuasive argument without referring to politics at all, and the questions that exam boards tend to set are those that theoretically can be accessed by all young people. However, a child will be much better placed to argue for or against the banning of smoking or the expansion of the local leisure centre if they understand the financial implications of doing so, the concept of the 'nanny state' and the wider impact of these decisions on society.

Preparing for creative and descriptive writing

Reading, of course, provides fertile ground for writing, but it can be challenging to organise our curriculum to give children the opportunity to develop both skills. In chapter 16, I suggest ideas for how to create a reading and writing culture, and this can be foregrounded within the 'library lesson'. In every library lesson, children can be given an extract from a text that ties into the genre of study in English lessons, and then invited to produce a piece of creative writing inspired by an image connected to that extract. This task is designed to build young people's confidence in appreciating the tropes of a particular genre and the vocabulary associated with it. Most importantly, the low-stakes environment provides them with a chance to play around with language without worrying about whether what they are writing is 'right' or 'wrong'.

These short extracts of writing then form a portfolio from which they can draw inspiration as they move up through the school. An eager Year 7 student is often far less inhibited about creating characters and scenes than their more hormonal Year 9 or 10 counterpart. And although it can be logistically challenging to keep hold of work from Year 7 through to KS4, I would argue that a collection of creative writing ideas would be invaluable to a Year 9 or 10 student who finds it harder to connect with the more imaginative side of themselves. Although the English language exam provides tasks that can, in theory, be thought of 'on the spot', a child with weaker literacy skills will find this particularly challenging.

Jennifer Webb usefully writes about how to prepare students for creative or descriptive writing in her book *Teach Like a Writer*,[32] explaining that young people can walk into the exam hall 'holding hands with their character'. This is a perfect analogy to support those who struggle with that initial inspiration and generation of ideas. As a teacher, it can be really frustrating to know that a young person can produce some really lovely images in their writing but often freezes under exam conditions. Webb's analogy expresses perfectly how students can spend time before an exam generating ideas and planning out a description of a character who will appear in their writing, and how comforting it would feel to have this character by their side as they enter the exam hall.

32. Webb, J. (2020) *Teach Like a Writer*, John Catt

Generating ideas for an effective piece of descriptive or creative writing is obviously strongly connected to the knowledge that a child has to draw upon when they open up the exam paper. Explicit teaching of narrative structure is key, not because the student will produce an entire narrative in the exam, but because they will produce a moment within that narrative and they must precisely appreciate the features of that moment. The weakest creative writing, as I witnessed again and again when I marked as an examiner, is often characterised by an attempt to tell the entire story, and to race from the beginning through to the end with a number of plot twists and extensive dialogue in between. One of the most useful ways to illustrate this point is with Todorov's narrative structure, shown below.

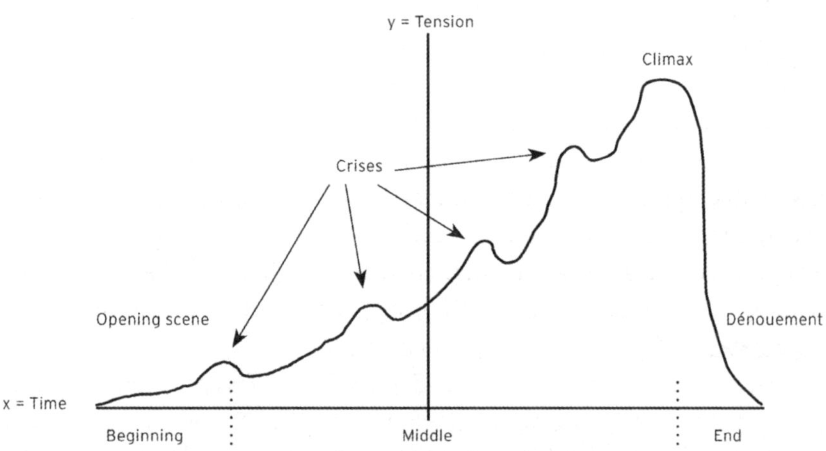

Only our most sophisticated writers are able to maintain a reader's interest from the beginning of a complex narrative through to the climactic point and the resolution. Occasionally, exam questions are designed so there is no other option but to write a whole story in 45 minutes. This can unfairly disadvantage our students, as they are encouraged into a writing trap that will not enable them to show off their true ability as writers. Wherever possible, young people should be encouraged to slow their writing down and focus on an opening or a key description. They must understand that the opening descriptions of setting and character are key, and that a 'story' can simply constitute a flashback or a memory that enables characters to discover something about themselves and move on with their lives. Such 'moments' can follow the narrative arc but allow for those rich and beautiful descriptions that even those who have experienced barriers to their literacy skills are able to demonstrate.

Overcoming literacy barriers

In chapter 1, I outlined my definition of children with low literacy skills. The English language GCSE offers those children who arrive at secondary school in a position of disadvantage to demonstrate that they have gained the ability to read and write independently after five years spent accessing our curriculum. This is an important goal for us as educators, as this qualification opens so many doors to post-16 study. The 'pass' in English on results day is a defining moment for so many, in terms of how they will view their competence in reading and writing as they move into adulthood. If they perceive themselves as being 'bad' at English, this feeling will follow them and affect the decisions they make about their lives. Persistent feelings of inadequacy in adulthood will also affect how they prepare their own children for school.

Of course, success stories abound about people who struggled at school but overcame their literacy barriers later in life, and determined that their children would not face similar obstacles. However, we have to accept that weaker literacy skills can be related to children's experiences of reading and writing at home; ultimately, there is a cycle of underachievement that follows particular families as they struggle to support their children and prevent them from experiencing the same difficulties. Some parents feel their children's literacy struggles are inherited and inevitable, as opposed to something that can be controlled. In the introduction to his book *Making Kids Cleverer*,[33] David Didau explains that he initially intended to write about the history of the research on genetics and inherited intelligence. But he found that the studies conducted in this area were

33. Didau, D. (2018) *Making Kids Cleverer: a manifesto for closing the advantage gap*, Crown House Publishing

problematic on so many levels that actually it was not worth dedicating a chapter to the topic. His book convincingly argues that children can be made 'cleverer' through the strategies I outlined in chapter 1: adopting a knowledge-rich curriculum, explicit instruction and meaningful practice. It is vital that, as educators, we do not set out with the fundamental belief that the children we teach are only as good as their prior attainment. Once barriers to literacy have been removed, prior attainment can become irrelevant, as children are finally able to access the academic world that was previously closed to them.

Chapter 4. Maths

The 'problem' with knowledge in maths

I studied maths at A-level and was perceived as one of those 'strange' students who liked both maths and English, as if they were two completely incompatible things. This didn't make sense to me: I loved both because they each offered me the opportunity to 'unlock' something powerful. If I read a book, I was entering into a world that gave me so much to think about, consider and apply to my own life. Similarly, each time I entered a maths lesson I felt I was learning something new about the world – unlocking a new rule or law or way of looking at something from another perspective. At primary school I had both reading books and maths books with questions to practise, like puzzles. It was fun to find the answers.

The purpose of this book, however, is to set out how each subject has its own unique discipline, and it is fair to say that the way you might prepare a student to learn the key knowledge and skills they need in maths is different from most other subjects. Although knowledge organisers can be useful, it is incredibly difficult to set out all the key mathematical concepts to be covered in a single unit, plus the corresponding examples needed for the concept to make any sense. Added to this, in order to truly 'know' how a concept works within maths, you must apply it. You can't simply answer questions on key characters as you might do in English. Instead, you must build up a sense of how to apply that concept repeatedly, and often in slight variations of the initial form as the questions increase in difficulty.

It is also very difficult to create a blanket knowledge organiser that would be appropriate to all students. Whereas in some subjects you can set a high ceiling and say that all students will learn a particular word or concept, 'knowledge' within maths generally operates in a much more linear/hierarchical fashion. If you don't have the foundation of knowledge in one thing, you don't stand a chance of being able to do something else that requires that knowledge as a prerequisite. It is also important to make connections between learning in different units, as one of the maths teachers at my school, Owen Gratton, has helped me to understand. For example, adding 10 + 10 + 20 uses the same skill as $p + p + 2p$, which is the same skill as root 3 + root 3 + 2 x root 3. It is one 'lot' of something, plus one 'lot' of something, plus two 'lots' of something. The more complex algebra is built on a strong base when the connection to more basic maths is made explicit, but that can be challenging to do on a single side of A4 paper.

I would also argue that the interplay between knowledge and skills is much more important within maths – for example, it is a *fact* that 5 x 6 = 30. There are key facts that we know and we apply them to develop the skill. Multiplying 12 x 43 x 54 requires the same skills as expanding $(x+2)(4x+3)(x+4)$. The skills need to be practised, but you are only able to do this if you have the procedural knowledge.

The diagram included opposite, developed by the National Centre for Excellence in the Teaching of Mathematics,[34] sets out this complex relationship and helps to demonstrate why knowledge organisers are less appropriate in helping students to make progress or 'achieve mastery' in maths. There is a tendency for some maths teachers to teach 'rules' like KFC (keep, flip, change) without an explanation of how to divide fractions. Although this may help students initially, particularly those who are weaker, it will make it harder for them further down the line when the 'rule' breaks down. Students need to be taught laws, procedures and methods, as set out in the NCETM diagram.

34. www.ncetm.org.uk/teaching-for-mastery/mastery-explained/five-big-ideas-in-teaching-for-mastery (accessed 19.09.20)

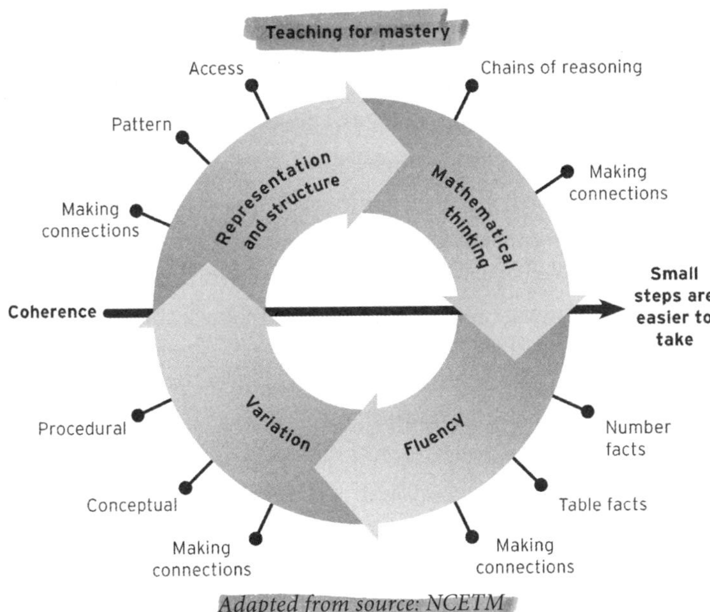

Adapted from source: NCETM

This is why, at Torquay Academy, learning key knowledge in maths is inextricably linked with practical application. We have bought into Sparx Maths[35] so that students' progress can be made sequentially and monitored closely. If a student comes up with an incorrect answer, the question will appear in future homework until they have mastered the approach. It is also particularly useful for procedures to be demonstrated and explained in maths, which is why we use Hegarty Maths[36] – it demonstrates the tasks that students are then expected to complete for homework.

Potential literacy barriers in maths

In maths lessons, disciplinary literacy is not about getting better at reading per se, but about getting better at interpreting questions: breaking them down into component parts and building those back up towards an answer. A key frustration among maths teachers is that students actually

35. https://sparx.co.uk
36. https://hegartymaths.com

do have the knowledge they need to answer the question, they just can't decipher what the question is asking them to do. Part of the problem can be the way in which questions are posed in maths papers. Take the example below:

On Wednesday, some adults and children were at the theatre.
The ratio of the number of adults to children was 3:2.
Each person had a seat in the Circle or had a seat in the Stalls.
3/4 of the children had seats in the Stalls.
55 children had seats in the Circle.
There are exactly 700 seats in the theatre.
On this particular Wednesday, were there people on more than 50% of the seats?

You must show how you get your answer.

Students who are stronger in maths than literacy and may be aiming for a grade 6 could be presented with questions like this:

1. Solve these equations:
   a. $4a - 7 = -20$ [2]
   b. $5(2x - 1) + 6x = 7 - 8x$ [3]
   c. $\frac{2}{x} = 4$ [2]
2. Solve algebraically the simultaneous equations:
   $3x - 2y = 10$
   $5x + 4y = 2$
   Show your working. [3]
3. a. The length of a string and the frequency of the note it produces are inversely proportional. A string of length 65cm is tuned to D, which has a frequency of 147 hertz (Hz).
   Calculate the length of string that would produce a note of frequency 110 Hz. [2]
   b. For a string of fixed length, the frequency of the note produced is directly proportional to the square root of the tension in the string. For a particular tension, the note produced is 196 Hz.
   What frequency note is produced when this is doubled? [2]
4. This is a drawing of a circle whose equation is $x^2 + y^2 = 25$ and a straight line.

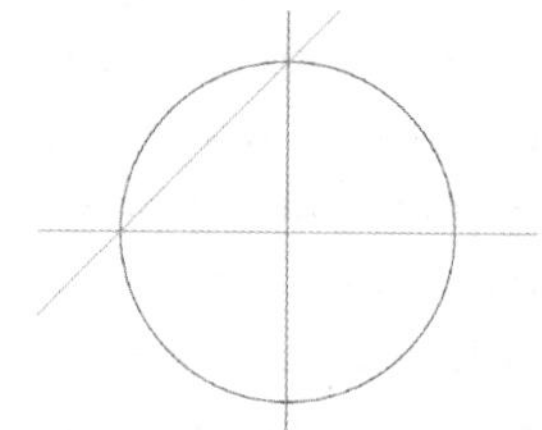

   a. Write down the equation of the straight line. [2]
   b. Use algebra to find the points of intersection of the circle and the straight line $y = x + 1$ [5]
5. Given that n is an integer, write down the next integer after n. Show that the difference between two consecutive integers squared is always an odd number - for example, $5^2 - 4^2 = 25 - 16 = 9$, which is an odd number. [4]

Had these questions been posed as algebraic symbols, the chances are that a far greater number of children would have been able to solve them. But many children are baffled by the way in which the mathematics is embedded within the dense vocabulary of the question. It almost feels like a hybrid of the two greatest challenges of their school careers: reading difficult words and performing complex mathematical equations. They also need to code the real world into the algebra, which for many presents a frightening mental barrier.

This barrier has come to be known as 'maths anxiety', where negativity towards the subject can be deeply ingrained from an early age as children come to associate maths with failure. The challenge is that often this culture of failure around the subject is perpetuated by other adults in school. Although most teachers would recognise that it would be unhelpful to refer to a dislike of reading, they do not apply this same logic to maths. Comments like 'You've lost me there, maths has never been my strong suit' are far too familiar. While children might hear adults talking about challenges they have faced with reading – and, crucially, how they overcame these barriers and went on to be successful – rarely do they hear adults outside the maths classroom talking about how they needed to solve a maths challenge in order to do their job and how rewarding they found it.

If a child complains to me about the relevance of maths to the real world, I always refer to my uncle, who wanted to move his staircase to make an extra bedroom upstairs. Trigonometry helped him to make the calculations that determined how much steeper the steps could be and therefore how much more space would be available. Usually, you would pay an architect a large sum to work this out, but it was actually pretty simple maths. There is not a single concept taught in maths that does not have relevance to the real world, because maths is an expression of the real world and how we have evolved to live within it. If every adult in school had a positive attitude towards maths, appreciating its relevance and beauty, then we would go a long way towards alleviating the anxiety felt by so many students.

Overcoming literacy barriers in maths

What can be done in the maths classroom to support students in improving their disciplinary literacy skills? Rosenshine's principles of instruction are probably more crucial in maths than in any other subject, as ultimately students will only get better through repeated exposure to expert modelling, the creation of shared class models, oral rehearsal and finally being given the scaffolds required to replicate the task independently.

Maths is also the subject where the creation of shared resources and workbooks can be most problematic. As discussed in chapter 1, PowerPoint can be a useful tool, but to a child with weaker literacy skills it can be infinitely more useful to have the information from a PowerPoint printed out and placed directly in front of them. The combination of workbooks and teacher exposition, using the visualiser to annotate and elaborate on printed material, can be incredibly powerful for students who struggle. Imagine the cognitive challenge of trying to copy down what is on a PowerPoint while simultaneously listening to a teacher's explanation and trying to process any new information (Craig Barton discusses this in his online course 'Making the most of worked examples'[37]). Textbooks are often used to provide the printed materials, but this can introduce an additional layer of complexity as a student ponders how to lay out their responses in their book so they look the same as in the textbook. This is more challenging when responses require diagrams to go alongside them – students may spend more time battling with rulers and pencils than actually figuring out the maths.

Maths teachers often use printed worksheets that set out the initial examples and then have a series of activities for students to follow, but the issue then arises of what to do with these worksheets once they have been completed. Even the most organised and efficient classroom will be interrupted as students stick work into their books, often never to be looked at again.

The problem with workbooks is that a maths teacher may not be able to predict exactly which gaps in learning will arise as they begin teaching a new topic. Whereas in English we can prepare a unit of work on *Lord of the Flies* that follows lesson by lesson, chapter by chapter, theme by theme, etc, depending on how the unit is arranged, in maths it is impossible to move on to more complex areas of trigonometry if students are still

37. Barton, C. 'Making the most of worked examples'. Retrieved from: https://craigbarton.podia.com/making-the-most-of-worked-examples (accessed 19.09.20)

struggling with basic algebra. A possible option is to create workbooks that attempt to follow each topic but provide space for 'enrich and embed' lessons. Students who are confident with the topic taught can spend time enriching their knowledge by applying it to new contexts or moving on to a more challenging area, while those who need to take a step backwards to embed prior learning more fully can use this space to do so. Mark McCourt, in his book *Teaching for Mastery*,[38] recommends using a Raising Attainment by Measuring Prior Progress (RAMPP) test at the start of each cycle. This facilitates the planning of extra lessons to go into blank pages when weaknesses are identified.

Just as across the subject disciplines there is not a 'one size fits all' approach to improving literacy skills, each maths class may not require the same approach to improving their capability within the discipline. An A-level further maths student is likely to cope perfectly well with a textbook, whereas for a Year 7 student in a nurture group this could prove a barrier; if that barrier were removed, they might be able to access the maths much more successfully.

Speak like a mathematician

For students with weaker literacy skills, the ability to orally articulate answers and the reasoning behind the answer is particularly important within maths. Unlike in written subjects, where expressing ideas orally can still be a barrier even when they have articulated them in writing, if a student is able to articulate their reasoning in maths then they are much more likely to be able to apply that reasoning in written calculations. An example of this could be: 'The answer is 28 because the angles on a straight line add up to 180 degrees and the calculation I did was…'. Such oral explanations will support the understanding of the class, so a teacher can plan to select key students to answer those questions that are particularly important to achieving success within the lesson. Students with weaker literacy skills can begin to catch up

38. McCourt, M. (2019) *Teaching for Mastery*, John Catt

with their peers if they are explicitly invited into the modelling and discussion process at key moments.

It is also important that staff are consistent in their use of language to describe key terms. There are many different ways to say 'subtract' – for example, 'take away' and 'minus'. Again, although it can be tempting to use the 'simpler' terms with weaker students, this can cause greater confusion down the line. If you use the term 'minus' to refer to subtraction and then go on refer to 'minus' numbers instead of 'negative' numbers, the opportunity arises for misconceptions. Students with weaker literacy skills *can* use the correct terminology and will be supported in doing so if the teacher models this in their expositions. This consistency applies not only to individual teachers with their classes, but also across the whole department. Dr Jenni Ingram refers to the significance of 'little' words within maths in a video created for the Association of Teachers of Mathematics.[39] She demonstrates how significantly meaning can be altered through small words, such as stating that something is 'the same' as something else.

Vocabulary is discussed in greater depth in chapter 14, but it is worth mentioning here how vital the precise use and understanding of terminology is in maths in particular. Applying inappropriate wording can lead to misconceptions, while failing to ensure that students have the correct grasp of key terms can be extremely problematic. In chapter 14 we will discuss the Frayer model more generally, but this graphic organiser for building student vocabulary is particularly useful in maths, owing to the power of the 'non-example'. For example, if the term is 'trapezium', it can be useful to look at shapes that are similar to reinforce the rules that must be met in order for a shape to be classed as a trapezium. This will also secure students' understanding of the term 'parallel' and how they can identify a trapezium by applying this knowledge.

Maths presents a vocabulary challenge, in that the mathematical definition of words may differ from the definitions they have encountered elsewhere. The word 'linear' can arise in art and science as well as maths,

39. Ingram, J. (2020) 'The words we use' (video), Association of Teachers of Mathematics. Retrieved from: https://youtu.be/g0WYJMLTYfk (accessed 19.09.20)

and although the general meaning is similar, each context requires a precise application of the term that those with weaker literacy skills may struggle to grasp unless it is explicitly taught and demonstrated.

Chapter 5. Science

The disciplines within the discipline

Science, of course, encompasses a number of disciplines. So, is it useful to ask a child to 'think like a scientist' when what we really mean is 'think like a physicist' or 'think like a chemist'? Perhaps it is helpful to go back to the EEF's visualisation of disciplinary literacy as a tree with wide-ranging branches (page 17); we can imagine that there are some fundamental elements that straddle the scientific disciplines, but that each has its own unique set of principles. It is also important to consider Daniel Willingham's assertion that novices do not think like experts,[40] and the implications of this when aiming to develop students' ability to think, read and write within a particular discipline.

In every school I have worked in there has been a healthy amount of banter among science staff regarding which discipline is ultimately the most significant/challenging/worthwhile. Such banter is fuelled by the passion each teacher feels for the unique properties of their own discipline. The most successful science departments are often those where expertise is maximised because each teacher is able to teach the discipline in which they are a specialist, especially at GCSE. At KS3, the benefits are less pronounced and, conversely, there are benefits to having teachers who are able to make cross-curricular links between the sciences and to build a relationship with a class over a sustained period of time. Timetabling constraints also mean that, in reality, science classes tend to have a single teacher.

So, before we consider how to improve the disciplinary literacy of science students, the first question to ask is: how genuinely literate are

40. Willingham, DT. (2009) *Why Don't Students Like School?*, Jossey-Bass

teachers within the specific scientific discipline they are teaching? Are biologists expected to teach physics lessons but given the bottom set, because being a non-specialist seems to matter less when you are teaching children who are not expected to reach a high level? Of course, I do accept that there are tiers within science and that it would be significantly more obvious to a high-ability class if they were being taught by a non-specialist. But I increasingly believe that we need the teachers who struggle the least to teach the students who struggle the most. For instance, when delivering a chemistry lesson on moles (see example below), it is crucial that the teacher has a clear and precise grasp of exactly what they are teaching. Although it is entirely possible for a non-specialist to gain the expertise needed to teach this concept, I have observed it being taught a number of times and it is one that young people, particularly those with weaker literacy skills, find particularly difficult. The interplay in this topic between algebra, the associated 'maths anxiety' and the scientific conceptual knowledge makes it challenging to teach.

H_2	+	I_2	→	2HI
1 mole of H_2		1 mole of I_2		2 moles of HI
6:02 x 10^{23} molecules of H_2		6.02 x 10^{23} molecules of I_2		12.04 x 10^{23} molecules of HI_2

Experts can appreciate more rapidly how and why a student may have arrived at a misconception and use this as an opportunity to model the correction to the whole class. A teacher attempting to deliver the lesson from a pre-prepared, centrally produced PowerPoint or resource will not have the dexterity of knowledge required to provide such precise and immediate feedback. Having said this, a 'non-expert' teacher who has worked hard to bring their subject knowledge up to speed will be well placed to appreciate the struggles of their classes and less likely to make assumptions about students' knowledge. So, of course, it is not the case that science teachers can only teach within their own discipline. But if a teacher is timetabled outside their specialism, this must be carefully considered and the teacher given the training required to deliver the content. It cannot be assumed that science teachers can be moved around the timetable indiscriminately.

Overcoming literacy barriers: breath and dexterity of knowledge

It is easy to underestimate the sheer volume of knowledge that underpins the science curriculum. The combined science GCSE specification contains around 200 pages – five times as many as the specifications for most other subjects. When we first introduced knowledge organisers across Torquay Academy, it was the science department for whom this posed the greatest challenge. We did not even attempt to squish everything covered in a learning cycle on to one side of A4; we settled on three pages, but even that felt like a compromise. Over time, similarly to maths, the science department has looked for ways to more efficiently facilitate each student's ability to self-quiz on the breadth of knowledge covered in the specification. The department uses the Tassomai app,[41] which the students have engaged with well, and we have expanded its use to other departments.

Paper-based study offers its own benefits in terms of broader literacy skills and viewing knowledge as part of a whole. But, although knowledge organisers offer a useful way to place knowledge at the heart of each curriculum, our science and maths teachers have been at the forefront of ensuring that students also have the opportunity to quickly and efficiently test their retrieval of a wider range of factual information. In science, as in maths, students need to develop the ability to quickly retrieve and apply knowledge in a variety of contexts. You only need to consider the number of different questions in a maths paper and a science paper to see that there is huge variation in how students are asked to present their knowledge. Let's compare this to English literature, where there are relatively few and (usually) relatively predictable questions. It is unsurprising that the correlation between weaker literacy skills and poor exam performance is stronger in science and maths than it is in English literature (but not English language, which is based on an unseen extract and offers no hiding places for weak readers). This trend was identified by GL Assessment in the *Read All About It* report:[42]

41. www.tassomai.com
42. GL Assessment. (2020) *Read All About It: why reading is key to GCSE success.* Retrieved from: www.gl-assessment.co.uk/whyreading (accessed 19.09.20)

GCSE subject	Correlation
English language	0.65
Geography	0.65
Maths	0.63
History	0.61
Science combined	0.61
English literature	0.60
Drama	0.57
Citizenship	0.56
German	0.55

Source: GL Assessment

In science, it is the breadth of knowledge combined with the dexterity of its application that can prove the greatest barrier to those with weaker literacy skills. Once again, what is required is expert modelling by an expert teacher, with key students invited into the shared class modelling discussion. This should be followed by plenty of practice, so that students can consider, when faced with a new problem, how they resolved a similar problem last time. This relates to Willingham's idea of the surface structure and deep structure of problems[43] and, of course, to direct instruction. It is important to remember that the exams sat by students at the end of their GCSE course are their opportunity to showcase their learning across their entire school career, and that the skill of making links between different areas of scientific knowledge cannot necessarily be truly exploited until the course content has been covered fully. This is where curriculum design in science can be particularly powerful, by allowing enough time for the course content to be 'completed' relatively early in Year 11.

'Covering' content is far from 'learning' content, and 'completing' the course content does not mean the course is finished and the curriculum is somehow narrowed. Rather, circling back over content leads to fresh appreciation and learning, as students make connections that it was not possible to make during the first teaching of a topic; they can secure their understanding and solidify key conceptual and procedural knowledge.

43. Willingham, DT. (2009) *Why Don't Students Like School?*, Jossey-Bass

Schools that struggle to allow time for this need to consider whether sufficient curriculum time is devoted to science. Given how fundamental scientific knowledge is to a range of other subjects at A-level and beyond, it makes sense to consider the number of options that students are studying and whether the breadth of options is undermining the depth of study. There is no subject where this question has greater relevance than science.

Ensuring that students have theoretically 'covered' the curriculum early on means that time can be devoted to what they find most challenging: making connections between their learning in each area and presenting this learning in a variety of unpredictable contexts. It is all about practice: relentlessly providing students with opportunities to grow their confidence.

The use of booklets within science

Our science department has found that workbooks/booklets have been key not only to ensuring the efficiency of curriculum delivery, but also to providing students with the opportunity to look back over their learning; they can quickly refer to past lessons to prompt them in their understanding of new concepts and ideas that link to those they have encountered before. As discussed in chapter 1, a child with poor literacy skills who uses a blank exercise book interspersed with worksheets is unlikely to find their own work a useful resource to revisit. This is particularly relevant in science, owing to the volume of content covered, the pace at which it is covered and the necessity of referring to prior learning to make sense of what comes next. A pre-printed workbook containing all the key content is far more likely to be treated with pride and respect by a child who appreciates the care and attention that has gone into making it, and is relieved by the removal of the painstaking trial of copying from the board.

Adam Boxer has written extensively on his blog about how to use booklets in science lessons.[44] There are benefits for all students, but

44. Boxer, A. (2019) 'Booklets: how I use them'. Retrieved from: https://achemicalorthodoxy.wordpress.com/2019/06/30/booklets-how-i-use-them (accessed 19.09.20)

booklets are one of few examples of a teaching methodology that can begin to roll back the cumulative disadvantage phenomenon. Whereas so much of what we change within education disproportionately benefits those who are already engaged and making excellent progress, booklets help to level the playing field for those who are falling behind. I discussed this in chapter 1 but it is worth reiterating here: booklets are one of the most powerful moves that any science teacher can make to support students who are struggling to access the curriculum.

Booklets are also a brilliant way to bring complex texts into science lessons. As Doug Lemov points out in *Reading Reconsidered*,[45] it is actually incredibly efficient to provide students with the key content of the lesson in a written format for shared reading guided by the teacher. It ensures that the key information is well presented and explained by the 'best expert' in the department, or possibly via a resource that is available externally. The resource can also directly address and pre-empt misconceptions. Adam Boxer has also written on his blog about how he carries out whole-class reading.[46]

Of all the subjects outside English, science is the most fruitful area for students with weaker literacy skills to make excellent progress. Not only is the knowledge so often relevant in texts that are read in other subjects, but that content can be delivered in a way that places reading complex texts at the heart of a lesson. At my school, we have just started working on an exciting project with our science team in which students with lower reading ages will have parts of their science lessons dedicated to improving their literacy skills. Rather than extracting students from lessons to undertake literacy interventions, the lessons themselves will become literacy-rich environments in which students can flourish without missing out on vital elements of their curriculum.

45. Lemov, D, Driggs, C and Woolway, E. (2016) *Reading Reconsidered: a practical guide to rigorous literacy instruction*, Jossey-Bass
46. Boxer, A. (2019) 'Whole-class reading: how I do it'. Retrieved from: https://achemicalorthodoxy.wordpress.com/2019/09/12/whole-class-reading-how-i-do-it (accessed 19.09.20)

Reading in science

- Is there a core 'story' to be told that relates to the topic? Can this best be explained through a dual-coded narrative or through a printed article that the teacher reads aloud and elaborates upon?
- Can all printed resources be collated in a booklet or workbook?
- Are students expected to read and retain chunks of writing from a PowerPoint slide?
- When reading complex texts, is the key vocabulary pre-taught to aid comprehension and retention?

Writing in science

- Do students understand how writing in science is different from other subjects?
- Are students provided with vocabulary banks to remind them of the key concepts that must be included within writing? Early on in students' learning journeys, writing should be about developing writing skills, not testing memory.
- Are writing tasks explicitly modelled to students, with the component parts broken down and explained (**I do**)?
- Are key students brought into the discussion that surrounds the whole-class creation of modelled writing (**we do**)?
- Are students given access to challenging writing tasks and the scaffolding they need to achieve success (**you do**)?

Sample vocabulary bank

The atmosphere

What do you know about the atmosphere and atmospheric pollution?
Use the words in the table to write extensively about the atmosphere.

1 point	2 points	3 points	4 points
nitrogen	photosynthesis	greenhouse gases	sulphur dioxide
oxygen	oceans	methane	nitrogen oxides
carbon dioxide	dissolved	short wavelength IR	high temperatures
volcanoes	sedimentary rocks	absorb	carbon monoxide
billions of years ago	fossil fuels	long wavelength IR	global dimming

Chapter 6. History

The power of history

History, at its heart, is a wonderful opportunity to engage students of all ability and literacy levels. It tells the story of who we are, how we came to inhabit this small island, the evidence of the past that we can see all around us and the impact of British people on the world. This subject, more than any other, offers children the chance to see themselves reflected. What complex chain of events led to someone like me living in this place? Why do I speak this language? What are the roots of the diverse words used in the English language and why is it so hard to learn? All these questions can, at least in part, be answered through the study of history.

History was my favourite subject when I was in Year 7. It was the last lesson on a Friday and I used to be genuinely sad when it ended, even though the freedom of the weekend beckoned. I still remember individual moments within those lessons – for example, the revelation that so much of our language is rooted in French as a result of the Norman conquest that began in 1066. I remember every moment of the Battle of Hastings as taught through what we now refer to as dual coding. My history teacher had a way of telling stories, of turning these complex events into narratives that I engaged with and cared about. Key characters were brought to life with all their strengths and weaknesses, and the impact of these traits on their decision-making and the historical events that followed was made clear. In his seminal work *Why Don't Students Like School?*,[47] Daniel Willingham explains why narrative experiences like these can be recalled in such vivid detail, while so many other facts are forgotten.

47. Willingham, DT. (2009) *Why Don't Students Like School?*, Jossey-Bass

It is interesting that the wording of one of the exam questions at GCSE is 'write a narrative account' – this has very precise requirements in terms of the expected content and how it is expressed. Although it can be useful to an extent to consider the crossover between writing a 'narrative account' in history and writing a narrative within English, it is far more useful to consider the differences in the requirements. A narrative within English requires imagination and detailed description, whereas a narrative account in history requires a precise appreciation of specific historical events. Marks are not gained through tangential description that does not further the aim of communicating specifically the chain of events that occurred at a particular moment in history.

So, how can learning history in and of itself be useful when tackling the literacy gap and the wider educational challenges often encountered by children with weaker literacy skills? Well, an appreciation of history is primarily an appreciation of identity. The teenage years are difficult to navigate and often even more challenging for children who struggle to fit in as a result of their weaker literacy skills. History offers the opportunity for children to appreciate the diverse landscape of British culture – to understand that a deep-rooted class and racial divide has resulted in societal inequalities that are still very much alive today. However, history also shows children that the most fundamental aspect of bringing about change within society is equal access to education. The value placed on education throughout history – as a route out of poverty for the disadvantaged – is an incredibly powerful message; history teachers are able to positively reinforce this message as a means of motivating those who struggle to see the 'point' of school. The bigger picture of education is one that many children will not have had drawn for them. Whereas their peers have grown up surrounded by books and an appreciation of the transformational power of education, those with weaker literacy skills may not have fully encountered this perspective. A history teacher therefore holds in their hands the power to spark a light of understanding in those children who may view education as something 'done to them', as opposed to something they can do for themselves in order to take control of their lives.

A knowledge-rich curriculum in history

There is much debate about the extent to which students should be trained to be 'historians', the pros and cons of this approach, and the relative merits of source work and discovery learning as opposed to direct instruction. In the humanities classroom more generally there has been a great deal of diversity in terms of the delivery of content at KS3. My own school, up until a few years ago, delivered a more homogenised 'opening minds' curriculum in which geography, history and RS were taught alongside each other under thematic headings. I can say from my own experience in our particularly disadvantaged context that this curriculum was not implemented in a way that facilitated success. The sweeping curriculum reform of 2013 resulted in many schools, including ours, moving to a more discipline-specific structure in order to better prepare students for the increased rigour of GCSE study.

Children with weaker literacy skills are best taught by teachers who have an exceptionally secure appreciation of their subject and a passion for it. In history, it is particularly important to appreciate how a solid grounding in key dates, events and their chronology forms the basis of understanding. A child with weaker literacy skills will find it very difficult to attempt to debate the relative merits of a particular source without a secure understanding of the events within which it is situated.

Michael Taylor has argued powerfully[48] for the need to train students in the basics of substantive historical knowledge before we even begin to think about training them to become historians. His argument brought to mind Kenneth Burke's comparison between an academic discussion and a parlour room conversation. Burke argued that we must listen and absorb the discussion before we attempt to join in.[49] Those who try to enter a conversation without first appreciating the flow of the discussion run the risk of looking foolish – they may make a point that has already been made or ask a question that has already been answered. Essentially, this is the position of our KS3 students when they enter the

48. Taylor, M. (2020) 'History at Michaela' in Birbalsingh, K (ed). *Michaela: the power of culture*, John Catt

49. Burke, K. (1941) *The Philosophy of Literary Form*, University of California Press

world of secondary history. It is the teacher's job to guide them into the conversation, but this is a complex role: there is much that these students need to know before they can begin to contribute. I believe this is why children with weaker literacy skills are often disengaged in the history classroom. Not only are they asked to navigate a number of different texts, but they are also asked to provide a critique that they will not truly be able to deliver until they reach university.

The argument that students should be taught a wide schema of knowledge, as opposed to that which can be traced directly from the exam, is made by Michael Fordham on his blog as he explores 'what makes a curriculum knowledge-rich'.[50] Essentially, this is what I am arguing for across all subjects. The broader a child's schema of knowledge (and consequently vocabulary), the stronger and more entwined the strands of their reading rope (page 18) will become. Rather than a cumulative disadvantage phenomenon, we have the reverse, particularly if schools capitalise on the opportunity to build a schema of knowledge across the curriculum. An especially powerful project could be one that places the knowledge students encounter across the curriculum into a broader schema or narrative referred to by each teacher when they introduce a topic. The Torquay Academy Dictionary, set out in chapter 14, is a good starting point because it identifies all the key words across subject areas.

Supporting students with weaker literacy skills

What has often struck me in the history classroom is the sheer number of pieces of paper. Children may have a range of source materials, a photocopied page of information from a textbook and a table into which they must then transpose 'key' information. In an attempt to support and engage children who struggle with extended reading and writing, knowledge is often spread over a number of different sheets and writing spread over a number of different boxes. This is not helpful to a child who struggles to navigate and organise themselves. Far more useful would be to

50. Fordham, M. (2016) 'What makes a curriculum "knowledge-rich"?' Retrieved from: https://clioetcetera.com/2016/11/19/what-makes-a-curriculum-knowledge-rich (accessed 19.09.20)

gather all the necessary materials into a booklet or workbook. The teacher can then, for example, use the visualiser to model the process of reading the text to identify the important information. Key students can be drawn into the conversation as the modelling progresses and children can then be given a specific amount of time to attempt the process independently. At this point, the circulation and support of the teacher is vital to identify misconceptions and shine a spotlight on work that has been done well.

I mentioned at the start of this chapter Daniel Willingham's assertion that children are more likely to remember facts when they are woven into narratives. This is particularly true for those children with weaker literacy skills. The history teacher has a unique opportunity to tell the story of a key historical moment through the guided reading of an account of the event. This is where PowerPoint might seem particularly alluring, because it allows us to interweave images and videos to illustrate the account. There is certainly a place for this, but when there are large chunks of information to impart, it is crucial for weaker readers to have this information printed out and placed in front of them. The teacher can then choose to highlight and annotate the text as they read, and to supplement the text with dual-coded diagrams that children don't have to copy down, but can sit and absorb. And, most importantly, remember.

Reading in history

- As with science, is there a core 'story' to be told that relates to the topic? Can this best be explained through a dual-coded narrative or through a printed article that the teacher reads aloud and elaborates upon?
- Can all printed resources be kept together in a booklet or workbook?
- Are students expected to read and retain chunks of writing from a PowerPoint slide?
- When reading complex texts, is key vocabulary pre-taught to aid comprehension and retention?

Writing in history

- Do students understand how writing in history is different from other subjects?

- Are students provided with vocabulary banks to remind them of the key concepts that must be included within writing? Early on in students' learning journeys, writing should be about developing writing skills, not testing memory (memory testing should be undertaken through regular, low-stakes quizzing).
- Are writing tasks explicitly modelled to students, with the component parts broken down and explained (**I do**)?
- Are key students brought into the discussion that surrounds the whole-class creation of modelled writing (**we do**)?
- Are students given access to challenging writing tasks and the scaffolding they need to achieve success (**you do**)?

Chapter 7. Geography

The cultural literacy of geography

I want to tell a short story that illustrates the geographical illiteracy that many teachers encounter on a daily basis. This is part of the wider cultural illiteracy that so many students struggle with and ultimately undermines their ability to read and write across the curriculum.

Early in my teaching career, when I worked at a school in a small Devon town, I organised a trip to London to see *Richard III* at the Globe theatre. I went about it in the way a teacher normally would back then and many still do now. I booked a coach, reserved the same number of tickets for the play as there were seats on the coach, and offered the places to students on a first-come-first-served basis. My head of department asked if she could offer the places to her top set first, as they would 'get the most out of it'. I politely declined. Actually, I'm not sure I was that polite. I felt strongly that all children should have access to this trip if they wanted to go. The letter to parents included a line that said financial assistance was available if needed; I had to argue for this as the trip wasn't actually 'essential' and the whole year group wasn't going. This was in the early days of pupil premium funding, when not many people really knew what it was and it effectively just plugged gaps in funding that had been cut from the SEN budget.

I was disheartened when no one took me up on the offer for financial assistance. Looking back, I understand how naive I was and the complex reasons why a child might leave a letter about a trip on their desk instead of taking it home, even if their teacher has enthusiastically explained that the price isn't necessarily fixed and they should speak to me about it privately. Of course they didn't. I'm embarrassed now that I thought they would.

As it turned out, there were two places left after the trip had been organised. I happened to have two boys in my class who particularly struggled; they were not typically known for their diligence, but recently they had been working really hard in lessons. I kept them behind one day and said that I had been looking for the two most improved students to reward – and it was them! The prize was a free ticket to see a play in London.

On the coach, the boys asked a barrage of questions. 'Is London in Devon?' 'Does the River Thames join up with the River Teign?' 'Will we see Highbury stadium/the London Eye/other famous UK landmark?' It's a cliche but it's true: it was very clear these boys had never left Devon. The driver was so charmed by their enthusiasm that he took a detour via Westminster so they could see all the sights.

There is plenty else I could say about that day that doesn't particularly relate to geography, but rather to the relationship between literacy and poverty that underpins everything this book is about. The boys had a field day moving around the pit at the Globe to get the best view of the action; I was mortified but the steward said it was great to see – that's exactly how the pit was designed to be used. Despite the fact that the trip lasted the whole day, the boys only had packed lunches and no money to buy an evening meal. We pretended that I was only lending them the money for a Burger King. We arrived home at 11pm and I stayed with the coach until all the students had been collected. Except, these two boys weren't collected and insisted they could walk home. I drove them home and made sure they went inside their houses.

Myriad factors were at play in the boys' lives, but it is not up to us, as geography teachers, to fix those factors. It is up to us to do everything we can to make sure they understand where London is in relation to Devon, how the river systems work in this country and so on. It is up to us to leave them better equipped to literally navigate their way around not just the UK, but also the rest of the world if that is what they choose to do.

A knowledge-rich geography curriculum and its relationship to GCSE English language

It might be anticipated that, as an advocate for literacy, I will suggest that geography is taught through written case studies, which can be read aloud by the teacher before they elaborate on key ideas. I certainly believe that this is a useful activity. However, before students attempt to access geographical case studies, they must acquire the fundamental conceptual knowledge that underpins the study of the subject. Grace Steggall has argued for the prioritisation of geographical literacy by foregrounding the teaching of fundamental geographical principles: 'key concepts, places, cultures, landscapes, and relationships between countries'.[51]

Once again we return to the idea that to understand any text, we must first appreciate its place in a broader context. This is incredibly relevant within the geography classroom. As in all subjects taught at KS3, foundational geographical knowledge will facilitate broader literacy benefits. The texts that students encounter in their English language papers could quite literally be set anywhere, and if we examine the 12 papers set by AQA since the new specifications in 2017, eight of them can be accessed far more easily with a firm foundation of geographical knowledge. The table overleaf lists the range of settings encountered by students in the AQA English language exams since June 2017. Mountain ranges have proven popular and students would be at a significant advantage if they were able to precisely imagine the perilousness and the beauty of the environment. A geography curriculum that provides this substantive knowledge will give weaker readers in particular the familiarity needed when conjuring worlds they have never physically encountered. We know that stronger readers are better equipped to deal with areas of text that they don't understand, circling back to these sections when they have a fuller grasp of the text as a whole. They are less likely to be put off by unfamiliarity. But weaker readers may lack this confidence and are more likely to give up on a text if they encounter too much unfamiliar vocabulary early on.

51. Steggall, G. (2020) 'Geography at Michaela' in Birbalsingh, K (ed), *Michaela: the power of culture*, John Catt

Exam	Setting	Geographical vocabulary/knowledge	Sample question
November 2019: fiction paper	Pyrenees mountain range, France	Pine resin Resort Mountain range Ridge A rumble in the mountains - indicates an avalanche and imminent danger Tsunami Termites	Evaluate how the writer makes the situation sound dangerous
November 2019: non-fiction paper	Burma, part of the British Empire, in 1922 (it is not mentioned that this country is now called Myanmar or whereabouts in the world it is located)	Bazaar Paddy fields Population An understanding of colonisation	How does the writer use language to describe the crowd of people?
June 2019: non-fiction paper	Atlantic Ocean A journey to Patagonia, a remote region in South America, in 1893	The ocean had continued to build Gusting at 40 knots Swell Frenzied conditions Breakers Horizon Churning surf Debris Gale Steamship Tremendous tumult of waters Perilous coast Tempestuous night	Use details from both sources to write a summary of what you understand about the different boats
November 2018: fiction paper	A prehistoric jungle	Jungle Hunting tiger, wild boar, buffalo, elephant Wilderness Safari Boulder Mountain avalanche	How has the writer structured the text to interest you as a reader?
June 2018: fiction paper	Oswald's Grammar School and places in the main character's imagination	Terraced house Ran like gazelles Prospector Nugget of gold	Evaluate how the writer conveys Mr Fisher's reaction to what he discovers
June 2018: non-fiction paper	A beach in California, US, in the 1950s Hilo, a town in Hawaii, in 1875	Manhattan Pier Surfing the morning glass Swell Shore Broadside Mahogany Plywood Pacific Ocean Ritual Native breadfruit tree Breaker and comber (definitions given) Tropical	Compare how the writers convey their different perspectives on surfing
November 2017: fiction paper	Pyrenees mountain range, France	Heat haze Tarmac Inhospitable Canvas awning Stone age village Excavation Boulder Archaeologist	How does the writer use language here to describe the mountain area?
November 2017: non-fiction paper	Crompton, a town in the North of England	Disadvantaged centre Northern industrial town Mean terraces Grim and forbidding, wasteland Derelict building Half-demolished houses Artefacts Squalid	Compare how the writers convey their different attitudes to the two schools

Of course, we could also analyse the exam papers in terms of historical, religious and scientific knowledge, and a substantive knowledge-based curriculum will support children's ability to read and access the texts they encounter across subjects. However, the geographical knowledge struck me to be the most significant in these papers, and even more so when the writing tasks are taken into consideration. One example of a creative writing task was 'Describe a place you think is beautiful'. Of course, the tasks are deliberately broad to allow for a wide range of responses. But those children who have been invited into the rich and varied global landscape offered by effective geography teaching will not only be able to draw on ideas of places, but will be able to deliver well-observed details that are a hallmark of effective writing.

Persuasive writing tasks often centre around debates that can be a central focus of geography lessons. In a paper that I have not listed in the table opposite, as the geographical knowledge was not central to the texts, cyclists outlined their experiences with reckless car drivers. The persuasive writing task that followed the comprehension questions was this:

> 'Cars are noisy, dirty, smelly and downright dangerous. They should be banned from all town and city centres, allowing people to walk and cycle in peace.'
>
> Write a letter to the Minister for Transport arguing your point of view on this statement.

It is not difficult to appreciate that a child with a firm understanding of urban development and planning is likely to be better placed to make well-reasoned arguments. Arguments that are, again, rooted in those details that set confident and articulate writers apart from those who struggle to develop their ideas.

The broader power of geography to motivate and inspire

A study of geography allows young people to observe their relative privilege in relation to the rest of the world. I have read texts aloud in which a child walks for miles to get to school, only for students to make comments such as, 'Oh my god, how could he be bothered?' This question exposes such ignorance regarding the value and power of education. In English, we might encounter a text like this only briefly, so it can be challenging to fully explore the relative economic situation of the particular nation. A fuller discussion could be had within the geography curriculum. For the development of a child's empathy, it is vital for them to consider the lives of the wide range of people who inhabit our diverse global landscape; they need to be able to place themselves in the position of a character or narrator, and not to feel alienated from them. Again, weaker readers are more likely to be put off if they encounter a character whose life feels vastly different from their own; it can act as a further barrier to their comprehension. Stronger, more experienced readers will be accustomed to dropping in and out of different worlds, and better equipped to see the world from an alternative perspective. The role of the geography teacher can be to open the door to these perspectives.

Effective literacy instruction in geography

There is a great deal of overlap between effective literacy instruction in geography and in science, and the arguments that I made around the use of workbooks in science (see chapter 5) can equally be applied to geography. The key distinction is in the level of comprehension of extended written materials that are key to accessing the most recent geography papers. As I mentioned in chapter 5 (pages 81-82), GL Assessment's *Read All About It* report[52] places the correlation between reading comprehension and success in geography as equal to that in English language and higher than in other subjects, including science:

52. GL Assessment. (2020) *Read All About It: why reading is key to GCSE success.* Retrieved from: www.gl-assessment.co.uk/whyreading (accessed 19.09.20)

GCSE subject	Correlation
English language	0.65
Geography	0.65
Maths	0.63
History	0.61
Science combined	0.61
English literature	0.60
Drama	0.57
Citizenship	0.56
German	0.55

It is not difficult to appreciate why this is the case, when a paper can typically be nine pages of text that students are expected not only to comprehend, but also to read through the lens of a geographer. They must evaluate key facts and present a reasoned argument in response to an extended question about an issue relating to the topic.

So, not only are students expected to digest such lengthy materials, but they must also construct a piece of writing that uses language appropriate to geographical writing. Students receive marks for spelling, punctuation and grammar, so it is important in geography teaching, at appropriate moments, for writing to be marked for accuracy. However, when you consider the small proportion of marks available for spelling, punctuation and grammar, it is far more important that students have the confidence to express their ideas and are armed with strategies to help them overcome challenges they may face. For example, the nine pages of case material are incredibly useful in terms of the rich range of vocabulary that is there in print – and spelt correctly – for students to draw on. Training for this paper should involve the explicit modelling of how to fully exploit the material for useful vocabulary and key phrases. Students must read the questions before attempting to read the case study, so they know from the outset the critical lens through which they are viewing the material. For those with weaker literacy skills, a useful scaffold can be to build a bank of words and phrases that they can refer to when writing their response.

Reading in geography

- As with science, is there a core 'story' to be told that relates to the topic? Can this best be explained through a dual-coded narrative or through a printed article that the teacher reads aloud and elaborates upon?
- Can all printed resources be kept together in a booklet or workbook?
- Are students expected to read and retain chunks of writing from a PowerPoint slide?
- When reading complex texts, is key vocabulary pre-taught to aid comprehension and retention?

Writing in geography

- Do students understand how writing in geography is different from other subjects?
- Are students provided with vocabulary banks to remind them of the key concepts that must be included within writing? Early on in students' learning journeys, writing should be about developing writing skills, not testing memory (memory testing should be undertaken through regular, low-stakes quizzing).
- Are writing tasks explicitly modelled to students, with the component parts broken down and explained (**I do**)?
- Are key students brought into the discussion that surrounds the whole-class creation of modelled writing (**we do**)?
- Are students given access to challenging writing tasks and the scaffolding they need to achieve success (**you do**)?

Chapter 8. Religious studies

The powerful knowledge offered by religious education

Never has a subject been more marginalised, diluted and squeezed than religious studies. The statutory requirement to study the subject, rather than enhancing its status within the curriculum, has in many schools served to reduce its study to tokenism. It is often the first subject to be dropped when a student requires intervention and it receives a marginal amount of curriculum time, despite regularly being a subject for which students are entered at GCSE. So we have a strange paradox: RS is deemed so significant that there is a statutory requirement to study it, but not significant enough to be given the necessary time and space on the curriculum to do it justice.

This is particularly problematic in schools where a large number of students have weaker literacy skills. Peter Johnston refers to the comprehension test bias that exists in reading assessments owing to the differing levels of prior knowledge among students.[53] The inextricable links between literature, the arts and religion mean it is unsurprising that those children with a strong grounding in religious education are more able to navigate the unseen texts in their English language paper. These days, I am no longer surprised by the outcome when I ask students what a writer's intention might be when describing a character as 'snake-like'. Many are able to explain that the description implies the character is unpleasant, perhaps even untrustworthy, but few are able to specifically link this to the Devil and the story of the Fall in the Bible.

53. Johnston, P. (1984) 'Prior knowledge and reading comprehension test bias', *Reading Research Quarterly*, 19:2, pp.219-239

As a child, I attended Sunday school and had a children's bible that I read and enjoyed. I remember studying *Lord of the Flies* as a teenager, making so many connections to the story of the Fall and noticing the representation of Simon as a Christ-like figure. At the time, I thought I was able to make these inferences because I was 'good' at English, but now I understand that I simply had advantages because of the knowledge I'd gained elsewhere.

So, before we can consider the ways in which religious education can best be delivered for those children who struggle with literacy, we must first appreciate the centrality of religious education *to* literacy. One of the worst things a school can do for a child with weaker literacy skills is to extract them from religious education. Doing so removes one of the central components in actually helping them to get better at reading. It deprives them of an opportunity to gain the knowledge that underpins our literature and permeates our language.

A knowledge-rich curriculum in RS

Sarah James argues powerfully that RS teaching should begin with the Judeo-Christian tradition, which 'forms the traditional bedrock of ideas and assumptions both in Britain and the West',[54] and as far as possible build a chronological narrative from there. Logically, the narrative of religion cannot be separated from the wider narrative of history. The two speak to each other in ways that are infinitely helpful to a child with weaker literacy skills, for whom the small success of recognising a concept taught in another subject can provide the springboard for deeper engagement with the topic.

When it comes to linking or separating the subject disciplines, it often seems to be all or nothing. This has always been a mystery to me. As mentioned in chapter 6, humanities subjects are sometimes taught alongside each other under a broad banner such as 'opening minds'; teachers of all these subjects then teach this homogenised

54. James, S. (2020) 'Religious education at Michaela' in Birbalsingh, K (ed). *Michaela: the power of culture*, John Catt

whole. At the other end of the spectrum, we have schools that separate out the disciplines and ensure that, as far as possible, teachers are able to specialise. This is the approach I have advocated, but it does feel as if there should be more collaboration in terms of the curriculum taught within disciplines, and more explicit links signalled to students so they can build their wider schema of knowledge. This applies not only within the humanities subjects, but also in terms of their links to English literature and expressive arts. The vocabulary project that I will discuss in chapter 14 highlights just how many links there are, as evidenced by the number of times the same word was identified as central to the learning in different subjects. Sometimes the same word would be applied differently and this in itself offers a rich opportunity to deepen understanding.

Dawn Cox refers to the difference between disciplinary knowledge and substantive knowledge within RS.[55] She explores some of the challenges faced in terms of precisely defining the disciplinary knowledge, owing to the fact that RS is not studied in and of itself at academic levels. Cox suggests that it can be fruitful to train students in the theological and philosophical 'lenses' through which RS can be viewed; instilling this critical awareness will ultimately support their ability to respond successfully to key questions and ideas. The argument that 'there are no right or wrong answers' in RS chimes with the misunderstandings that can arise about effective criticism in English: there are definitely answers that are more 'right' than others, and providing even our weakest students with this disciplinary knowledge will facilitate their success at much higher levels. Attempting to encourage them by giving them a false belief that whatever they write will be 'OK' will only leave the weakest students struggling to come up with even the most basic argument.

Cox has also written a number of RS quiz books that foreground what she describes as 'substantive knowledge' – the content that sits at the heart of a knowledge-rich RS curriculum. Ensuring that all students are

55. Cox, D. (2020) 'It's all coming together – an introduction to the disciplines of RE'. Retrieved from: https://missdcoxblog.wordpress.com/2020/06/03/its-all-coming-together-an-introduction-to-the-disciplines-of-re (accessed 19.09.20)

well versed in this key knowledge will not just equip them to tackle the RS GCSE paper, but will also provide them with a useful grounding that will support them in their studies across the curriculum. But, more than this, our young people are far more likely to be successful in the school community and beyond if they understand Britain's vast and diverse religious landscape. Gaining a knowledge and appreciation of religious differences is central to the development of a young person's character, whichever cultural background they have been brought up within. What most struck me about the different religious texts when I studied RS was not the differences between them in terms of the central figures, customs or rituals, but the common theme that underpins the key ideas. It is a message of love, hope and the fundamental goodness that lies within us all. A study of religion can help to bring a school community together, and in a society that can often feel deeply divided, the power of this should not be underestimated.

Supporting students with weaker literacy skills

In a similar vein to English and history, the teaching of RS is often about telling stories. In fact, we could argue that religious stories form the basis of all stories and the storytelling tradition itself. The fundamental questions that humans began to ask about themselves at the dawn of time were answered with stories passed on through the oral tradition. Myths and legends about gods and goddesses were used to explain the very nature of our existence, and the tales that endured were those with the most powerful and memorable narratives. Teachers of RS have a unique opportunity to engage with those children who have rarely been told stories – those who struggle with the fundamental idea of a narrative, understanding characters and ultimately finding their own voices.

How a teacher chooses to tell these stories is key in supporting those with weaker literacy skills. These questions can support your thinking around this:

- Do I have a rich understanding of this story? Am I able to communicate the narrative in a way that brings out the central ideas that led the story to endure for centuries/millennia?
- If I am going to ask my students to answer questions/write about this story, will they have a hard copy in front of them or will I expect them to jot down notes?
- Can elements of the story be supplemented with dual coding/images of artwork in order to embed the key ideas and concepts?

Once again we come back to the allure of the PowerPoint. Although this is a really useful tool to project images, if PowerPoint is used to tell a story then a child with weaker literacy skills will be less likely to engage with it, particularly if the slides are covered with words that the teacher reads and students are expected to 'make notes' from. Just as I have argued for in other subjects, a booklet or workbook of key resources will provide literacy-rich classroom materials that support reading progress, particularly if the teacher reads the text aloud, elaborates on key ideas and explicitly pre-teaches vocabulary and central concepts.

Case study: Dawn Cox

'Rather than shying away from foreign language words, we should make a "thing" out of them,' Dawn says. 'Telling students words in Hebrew, Sanskrit, etc, makes them feel clever. I also verbalise them in context repeatedly and write on the board to get students confident in hearing and seeing them. Whole-class recall can help them say it themselves. The kids love learning these words.

'This also links to explicitly unpicking etymology. I do this a lot so students can see the roots of words, which means they develop their decoding skills further.'

Dawn's free booklet for Oxford University Press, *Closing the Word Gap: activities for the classroom, religious education*, can be downloaded at: tinyurl.com/yyx229fb

Reading in RS

- Pre-teach key concepts and vocabulary before tackling texts.
- Use booklets of key resources and materials that students can refer back to.
- Carry out regular quizzing on key knowledge needed to make sense of reading material.

Writing in RS

- Ensure students are well versed in the 'critical lenses' that will allow them to form cogent arguments.
- Provide the weakest students with the scaffolds they need to achieve the highest grades. Don't simplify the task – give them the resources they need to reach the top. These can include writing stems and frames that give them a 'feel' for what academic writing is like in this subject.
- Include regular practice of the components of extended writing and frequent opportunities to piece these parts together.

Chapter 9. Expressive arts

There is a common misconception that children with weaker literacy skills can use their expressive arts lessons as a way of 'escaping' their literacy struggles and gaining freedom of expression. Although it is true that some children are successful in art, music or drama in spite of their literacy difficulties, it is far more common for children with weaker literacy skills to struggle with these subjects as much as any other. Children from poorer socioeconomic backgrounds are also far more likely to have limited access to the arts outside school, and in schools that are more economically disadvantaged they are less likely to participate in extracurricular activities that provide access to cultural experiences. And then there's the fact that expressive arts lessons are among those from which children are likely to be extracted for literacy interventions.

Once again, we see the cumulative disadvantage phenomenon in action. There is a wealth of research evidence that connects access to the arts with academic attainment.

Key research findings of the Cultural Learning Alliance (2017)[56]

- Participation in structured arts activities can increase cognitive abilities by 17%.
- Learning through arts and culture can improve maths and English attainment.
- Learning through arts and culture develops skills and behaviour that lead children to do better in school.
- Students from low-income families who take part in arts activities at school are three times more likely to get a degree.

56. Cultural Learning Alliance. (2017) *Key Research Findings: the case for cultural learning.* Retrieved from: https://culturallearningalliance.org.uk/wp-content/uploads/2017/08/CLA-key-findings-2017.pdf (accessed 19.09.20)

- Employability of students who study arts subjects is higher and they are more likely to stay in employment.
- Students from low-income families who engage in the arts at school are twice as likely to volunteer.
- Students from low-income families who engage in the arts at school are 20% more likely to vote as young adults.
- Young offenders who take part in arts activities are 18% less likely to re-offend.
- Children who take part in arts activities in the home during their early years are ahead in reading and maths at age nine.
- People who take part in the arts are 38% more likely to report good health.

A 2012 report from the National Endowment for the Arts in the US showed that, by nearly every indicator studied, students of low socioeconomic status (SES) who had arts-rich educational experiences significantly outperformed their peers from low-arts, low-SES backgrounds, closing (and in some cases eliminating) the gap that often appears between low-SES students and their more advantaged peers.[57]

Although much of this research focuses on the enriching experiences offered by the arts and the fostering of creativity, I would also argue that the arts help to build the rich schema of knowledge that supports literacy success. The tension between 'knowledge' and 'creativity' is another false dichotomy that has plagued our profession over several decades. The notion that encouraging children to learn factual information involves a return to colourless and uninspiring 'Gradgrind' lessons could not be further from the truth, particularly when it comes to expressive arts. Knowledge can also be developed through the experience of listening to Pachelbel's *Canon in D Major* and exploring why it has become such a popular wedding song. The visual elements of art can be taught through the work of artists who are distinguished in a particular skill – for example, William Morris and his skill in pattern design. The work of

57. National Endowment for the Arts. (2012) *The Arts and Achievement in At-Risk Youth: findings from four longitudinal studies.* Retrieved from: https://www.arts.gov/sites/default/files/Arts-At-Risk-Youth.pdf (accessed 20.10.20)

Morris opens up a cross-curricular body of knowledge that includes his attitude towards the Industrial Revolution and the decline of the 'craftsman' in the face of industrial production.

Tracing the history of art, music and drama through the ages gives young people another lens through which to further their learning in history, geography, RS and literature. The connection between art and science is clear through, for example, the work of Leonardo da Vinci, and tracing this connection can help young people to appreciate the great inventions of the modern age. This, in turn, links to technology and the rise of the entrepreneur, illustrating how a strong foundation in knowledge, innovation and creativity is needed from across the curriculum in order to move the human race forward. The ethics of this are explored within literature and RS, and the consequences within geography and science.

Chapter 10. Technology and related subjects

The world of enterprise brought into the classroom

What has always struck me about technology classrooms is the way in which children continually make links between the knowledge they are learning and the real world. Often this knowledge is applied in a very literal sense – taking home a chair or a bird box that they have made, for example, or a meal they are proud to show off. The best technology departments start by supplying students with a 'brief'. This will vary in length depending on the subject, but it will essentially provide the background information for a task that needs to be completed and situate this task in a believable context. For example, in construction, a student will be given a detailed client brief to decipher and tasked with putting together a proposal for a building project that will meet the client's expectations. In business studies, students may have to draw up a business plan complete with profit and loss forecasts. In catering, a brief will again be provided and students must demonstrate their ability to prepare on-budget meals that meet their client's needs.

Technology and related subjects are therefore an excellent opportunity for students to appreciate how vital literacy skills are in any workplace. If they do not plan to go on to university after school, they may well see essay-writing skills as irrelevant to their future career. They may find relative safety in those classrooms geared towards skills beyond reading and writing, and it is really important that they have the time and space to nurture these skills. But the teachers of these subjects often hold the key to unlocking the literacy potential of their students – they are in a position to harness this engagement. Through the guided reading of key texts that will enhance students' knowledge in the subject area, teachers can provide an opportunity for them to experience reading in an environment they can be successful in.

Owing to the incredibly diverse nature of the subjects within this discipline, it would not be appropriate here for me to write a 'catch-all' section about how to support students of low literacy. These subjects each involve a unique blend of maths, non-fiction writing, science, humanities and expressive arts, alongside other subject-specific elements. I hope that the teaching approaches outlined elsewhere in this book offer ideas that are relevant to the teachers of these subjects, giving them the confidence to apply literacy strategies that will work in their classroom – and to resist those that will not.

Chapter 11. Media studies

The removal of media studies from compulsory study

In the curriculum reforms made to the English language GCSE for first assessment in 2017, the study of media was essentially removed. All non-fiction texts were to be printed articles or extracts, as opposed to the previous inclusion of texts from blogs, websites and magazines. In the past, part of the body of knowledge to be taught in English concerned 'presentational features': how a text could be manipulated to express a particular viewpoint through the use of images, layout, colour, fonts, etc. Although I have been broadly in favour of these curriculum reforms, and the reforms made to the media studies GCSE, I do feel that young people are now leaving school without the exceptional critical awareness required to navigate an increasingly complex media landscape.

Students with weaker literacy skills are far more vulnerable to the twisting and spinning of reality according to the political or economic position of the producer of a media text. Couple this with the lack of specific historical, political or economic knowledge required at KS3, or within the core subjects at KS4, and an increasing gap is developing between those who leave school well equipped to enter and participate in a democratic society and those who do not.

This is particularly significant in the light of a number of media scandals over the past decade. The Leveson inquiry of 2012 brought into sharp focus the threat to a free and democratic society when the relationship between the government and the media becomes too close. These issues resurfaced during the Brexit campaign of 2016 and the US election campaign in the same year. The Cambridge Analytica data scandal of 2018 highlighted just how susceptible young people are to marketing and political canvassing targeted to their demographic profile and interests. Now more than ever we need to educate young people to be hyper-vigilant and critical of the media they consume.

Many young people grow up in households where the media is treated with a healthy dose of scepticism, but what does it really mean to be sceptical of 'the media'? How informed is this scepticism in terms of who is producing a particular news story and its reliability? Donald Trump is well known for his declarations of 'fake news' whenever a story breaks that does not portray him in a positive light. How are young people to know that the media derided by Trump is actually firmly rooted within democracy and freedom of speech? How are they to know that the free press was a breakthrough for the working classes, and that the job of holding the government to account is important and powerful? This message has been lost because it is only taught to those children who specifically choose to study media studies at KS4, or whose school happens to incorporate this teaching into English or history, or into a tutor, PSHE or citizenship curriculum.

There are two points in the PSHE curriculum[58] that link to what is described as 'digital literacy':

> *'L26. that on any issue there will be a range of viewpoints; to recognise the potential influence of extreme views on people's attitudes and behaviours.'*

> *'L23. to recognise the importance of seeking a variety of perspectives on issues and ways of assessing the evidence which supports those views.'*

Schools will all implement PSHE in different ways and with different specialist teachers. Some will have timetabled lessons with a range of staff delivering content; others will have timetable collapses throughout the year featuring invited guests. The main focus of the first objective listed above relates to the potential for extremism and indoctrination, which are

58. www.gov.uk/government/publications/personal-social-health-and-economic-education-pshe Please note: updated statutory guidance came into effect in September 2020

the most severe consequences of a range of factors that improved media literacy could go some way towards tackling.

If the English language curriculum were to be reviewed again, as I am sure it will be at some point, I believe the removal of the study of media needs to be reconsidered. I welcome the increased vigour of all the qualifications, but in this instance a balance could have been struck between print-based articles and those a young person is more likely to actually encounter in their everyday life.

Media studies for students with weaker literacy skills

Media studies has often been advocated as a 'soft option' for students with weaker literacy skills. I outlined some of the history of the qualification in chapter 2, but one of the most interesting experiences for me in this area came about 10 years ago, when I was attempting to teach the media GCSE paired with the English GCSE instead of literature. Back then, this was seen as the 'easier' way for some young people to gain the additional qualification in place of literature. It was a resounding failure. It wasn't that the exam was any harder, particularly – it was more the sheer volume of coursework combined with the specific knowledge required for students to be successful, which lay outside the typical domain of an English teacher.

The new media studies specifications for GCSE and A-level have been incredibly valuable in laying out precisely which theorists and theoretical frameworks need to be taught in order to prepare students for the exam. This opens up an excellent opportunity for cross-curricular links to be made when it comes to the teaching of English literature, English language and, often, business studies and history. Media studies is far from a 'soft option' for young people with weaker literacy skills, but the explicitness of the exam specification combined with the option to carry out a 30% non-examined assessment does make it a viable option – and an important one in terms of the arguments expressed in the first part of this chapter.

Alongside the specific theories laid out in the specification, there are close-study products that carry with them their own body of knowledge.

These can be tricky for media studies teachers to prepare for because the shared central resources or text books often do not exist. In my experience, it is much more challenging to prepare a lesson on the French TV drama *Witnesses* than it is to prepare a lesson on *Frankenstein*, as there is nothing in the way of study guides and online discussion. Although it is important to allow students to form their own responses to the close-study products, it is also vital to model successful responses and analysis. The 'I do, we do, you do' process is as important in media studies as it is in any other subject, although it can be tempting to believe that it is less necessary because students tend to find it more straightforward to generate ideas when it comes to media products. This can be a double-edged sword, however, as although students with weaker literacy skills might be more prepared to record their responses, the quality of the response needs to be carefully scaffolded. It is so easy for students to fall into stream-of-consciousness responses that will undermine their ability to pick up vital marks.

Of all the subjects and qualifications I have taught over the past 15 years, generating discussion around media products (particularly moving image products) is what I have found most enjoyable. Young people can feel alienated from the printed word, but they feel comfortable with media products and it is a privilege to discuss with them their ideas and interpretations of characters, themes and directorial intention. For many, this confidence can serve to build a bridge to English literature, as many of the tools of analysis are similar. The framework that I outlined in chapter 2 is very similar to the one we use in media studies at Torquay Academy, so that we can capitalise on the analytical structure that is familiar to both subjects. This is particularly valuable for students with weaker literacy skills.

I have talked a lot about booklets and I will not repeat the arguments here. Instead, I will express my belief that, within media studies, it is important to invest in printing *colour* booklets (printing companies can be flexible in allowing booklets to be printed in a mixture of black and white and colour). In order to fully appreciate the close-study products, students must be given access to them in hard copy and in colour – looking at them on screen is just not enough for those with weaker literacy skills or possibly SEN (discussed in chapter 17). Booklets are ideal for providing stills of key moments in moving image products, and it is important that young people are able to refer to these in their exam, as well as to sections of dialogue or the screenplay. Screenplays are excellent resources for young people with weaker literacy skills, who might struggle to follow dialogue or grasp complex storylines on screen. We might assume that students can automatically follow what is happening on screen, but when characters are similar in appearance, or when dialogue is mumbled or loud music is playing, the action can be hard to decipher. Subtitles can be useful, but they disappear very quickly and sometimes, as in a book, we want to revisit past events to check our understanding.

Chapter 12. Physical education

The PE department is often either exempt from literacy expectations or expected to follow whole-school initiatives that are impractical in a sports environment. Once again, what is needed is an approach that takes into account the context of the subject. Literacy needs to be introduced in a way that is useful in securing an understanding of the key concepts and helps to improve students' literacy levels.

Clearly, once we reach KS4, many of the principles outlined in chapter 1 can be usefully applied to classroom-based lessons. There are many similarities between PE and biology in terms of the technical content and written skills, and the same arguments can be applied regarding the use of booklets. I would recommend that teachers of PE at KS4 read chapter 5 for specific ideas relating to this.

Let's focus here on the nuts and bolts of a practical lesson in a physical environment, whether it is in the sports hall, on the football field or on artificial grass. PE provides an excellent opportunity to develop vocabulary, particularly technical vocabulary relating to the human body and its response to exercise. Warm-ups and stretches can be used to focus on different muscle groups; key terms can be taught explicitly and students invited to practise using those terms in class discussions. Anatomical terminology is useful for the further study of PE and biology, as well as providing that crucial background knowledge that is key to literacy. Just as strong geographical knowledge helps to facilitate a student's understanding of settings in unseen fiction texts, anatomical knowledge can support students in making inferences from character descriptions. It can be easy to take for granted that a child with weaker literacy skills will understand the terms 'limb' or 'shin', but lacking this knowledge will place them at a significant disadvantage when it comes to deciphering character descriptions.

Students with weaker literacy skills are often extracted from PE lessons to attend additional literacy lessons. This can be counterproductive, particularly if PE is a subject that the student enjoys and can be successful in. A far greater impact could be had if tier 2 and 3 vocabulary were identified within the PE curriculum and taught explicitly, revisited and embedded over the five years of the student's physical education.

Chapter 13. Modern foreign languages

The argument is often made that a child should not learn a second language if they are unable to read well in English. It is certainly the case that a child who struggles with literacy in their own language is likely to find it more challenging to acquire an additional language. In his book *Closing the Vocabulary Gap*,[59] Alex Quigley explores the benefits of an expansive vocabulary in English to acquiring a new language. As we have seen time and again in this book, a barrier in literacy is likely to be a barrier to progress in any subject.

A typical curriculum model may identify students who have weaker literacy skills and immediately strip modern foreign languages from their timetable in favour of additional literacy support. It is understandable that school leaders might favour such curriculum models, but removing access to MFL entirely can have unintended consequences for students' literacy progress.

If we consider Scarborough's reading rope once again (page 18), the background knowledge acquired through the study of another language is considerable. At a fundamental level, understanding another culture and tradition is key to recognising our own place in the world – I would argue that it is vital for a child to be exposed to another language in order to hold up a mirror to their own lives. Developing the ability to express themselves in another language also opens up doors of opportunity that will forever remain closed if they do not have the confidence to ask straightforward questions or say something simple about themselves. Many of the students I teach have never been abroad; if they are not exposed to another language, they may feel that travelling and experiencing other ways of life are just not an option for them.

59. Quigley, A. (2018) *Closing the Vocabulary Gap*, Routledge

In addition to the wealth of background knowledge acquired through language learning, there is a growing body of evidence that learning a second language can actually improve a child's ability to access their first language. Murphy et al. (2015) found the following in their study of Year 3 children:[60]

> *'This study investigated whether learning a second language (L2) has a facilitative effect on first language (L1) literacy and whether there is an advantage to learning an L2 with transparent grapheme-phoneme correspondences. One hundred fifty Year 3 children were randomly assigned into one of three groups: L2 Italian, L2 French, and control. Children were pretested on measures of English (L1) spelling, reading and phonological processing. The L2 groups then received 15 weeks of L2 instruction in Italian or French, respectively. The L2 groups outperformed the control group on post-test measures of English reading accuracy and different aspects of phonological processing. In addition, there was an advantage for the L2 Italian group as their scores were higher than the L2 French group on English reading accuracy and phonological processing.'*

This study typifies findings in this area and there are a number of possible reasons for this 'facilitative effect'. One is the number of cognates encountered – words in different languages that have similar roots (the process of breaking a word down into its constituent parts and establishing the root is common practice in MFL). A student is likely to be encouraged to look for the parts of the word they do understand and then infer the meaning within the context of the sentence. This skill, explored further in chapter 3, is fundamental to vocabulary acquisition.

Another potential reason is the effective deployment of oracy instruction in MFL classrooms. Oral rehearsal of new vocabulary is fundamental

60. Murphy, VA, Macaro, E, Alba, S and Cipolla, C. (2015) 'The influence of learning a second language in primary school on developing first language literacy skills', *Applied Psycholinguistics*, 36:5, pp.1133-1153

to the pedagogical approach, as is the requirement to build listening skills within conversation. MFL teachers have been using many of Doug Lemov's *Teach Like a Champion* approaches for decades: the structured turn and talk, oral rehearsal of new words, routine drilling of key knowledge and terms. In essence, MFL is the original 'knowledge-rich' curriculum – the original deployer of spaced retrieval practice as new vocabulary builds upon the foundational learning of basic conversational structures.

An interesting avenue of research is opening up into the relationship between improvements in cognitive brain function and bilingualism. This is far beyond my area of expertise, but it is a useful area for further research for school leaders who are making challenging decisions regarding the curriculum for students furthest behind with their literacy skills. Ultimately, if all teachers take on the role of teacher of literacy, the exponential benefits will be such that these tough decisions won't need to be made.

Part III
Whole-school approaches to improving literacy

Chapter 14. Explicit vocabulary teaching and the TA Dictionary

The growth of explicit vocabulary teaching

Over the past few years, a revolution in vocabulary teaching has begun in Britain's secondary schools. The influence of Isabel Beck et al.'s *Bringing Words to Life*[61] on US schools was significant almost two decades ago and the Education Endowment Foundation drew on their research for its Closing the Gap workshops across UK schools in 2013-14. A central focus of these workshops was highlighting the levels of complexity of the words encountered by students in lessons, and the associated need to robustly and explicitly teach the more challenging words. This idea began to take root at a grassroots level.

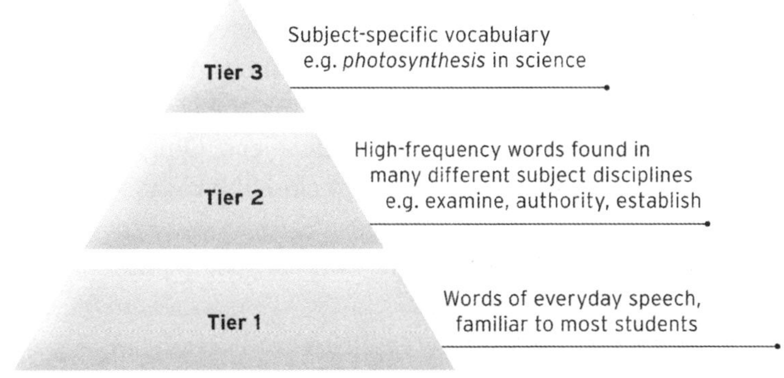

Adapted from source: Kingsbridge Research School

61. Beck, IL, McKeown, MG and Kucan, L. (2002) *Bringing Words to Life: robust vocabulary instruction*, Guilford Press

After Doug Lemov's success in bringing *Teach Like a Champion* ideas to the UK through conference-style workshops, his *Reading Reconsidered* team offered conferences that specifically explored the teaching of reading. I attended one of these workshops in 2016 and explicit vocabulary teaching was a central focus. Most useful was the notion of 'pre-teaching' vocabulary. Typically, when reading a text with a class, a teacher waits until a challenging word is encountered and pauses at that point to discuss possible definitions and draw on the prior knowledge of the students. The flaws of this approach were made clear in the workshop I attended (and in the *Reading Reconsidered* book[62]): it is incredibly inefficient and can lead to misconceptions. Students can reach a higher level of understanding of the text if they already know the meaning of these challenging words. So, key words should actually be introduced to students at the start of the lesson to allow for a more efficient study of the text.

The influence of the work of ED Hirsch Jr on UK education policy has brought to the fore the notion of vocabulary size as a proxy for wider educational attainment and ability. This, coupled with growing recognition of the cumulative disadvantage phenomenon, has brought vocabulary instruction to the forefront of many headteachers' minds when it comes to school improvement. Probably the most influential book in this area in UK education has been Alex Quigley's *Closing the Vocabulary Gap*.[63] This book struck just the right note with school leaders and classroom teachers by considering the issue of educational disadvantage through an incredibly practical lens. Quigley advises that schools should take the following steps to close the vocabulary gap:

- Train teachers to become more knowledgeable and confident in explicit vocabulary teaching.
- Teach academic vocabulary explicitly and clearly, with coherent planning throughout the curriculum.

62. Lemov, D, Driggs, C and Woolway, E. (2016) *Reading Reconsidered: a practical guide to rigorous literacy instruction*, Jossey-Bass
63. Quigley, A. (2018) *Closing the Vocabulary Gap*, Routledge

- Foster structured reading opportunities in a model that supports students with vocabulary deficits.
- Promote and scaffold high-quality academic talk in the classroom.
- Promote and scaffold high-quality academic writing in the classroom.
- Foster 'word consciousness'.

The Torquay Academy Dictionary

After the publication of *Closing the Vocabulary Gap*, staff members at Torquay Academy created our own dictionary, which aims to address each of Quigley's guidance points. The TA Dictionary is very much a collaborative effort. It is an attempt to give our students access to the tier 2 and tier 3 vocabulary they need in order to be successful. in all their subjects across the curriculum. It contains more than 2,000 words, definitions and etymological origins.

Purpose of the dictionary

I was given the 'vocabulary project' by our principal, Steve Margetts. In collaboration with our head of English, Jen Brimming, he had come up with the idea that we should have a book of all the words our young people needed to know. We had all been influenced by Lemov's *Reading Reconsidered* and Quigley's *Closing the Vocabulary Gap*; Jen had also been an examiner for GCSE English literature and had been struck by the way in which a candidate could immediately position themselves as likely to obtain the highest bands through their selection of appropriate and useful vocabulary. It can be very difficult to pin down exactly what gives these maximum-mark answers their 'flair' and 'cogency', but there is one feature they all share and that is wide, appropriately selected vocabulary.

The context of Torquay Academy is one in which we must do everything we can to provide our young people with the equipment they need to climb the 'curriculum mountain', a topic I have written about on my blog.[64] Explicit vocabulary teaching was highlighted in a recent EEF report[65] as the second most effective method of improving literacy in schools, after disciplinary literacy (although I would argue that explicit vocabulary teaching is part of disciplinary literacy).

Background: Word of the Week

In English, Jen had already introduced 'Word of the Week', following the explicit vocabulary model set out by Lemov in *Reading Reconsidered*. Below is a sample piece of student work that illustrates the impact of Word of the Week; this child had previously struggled with written expression.

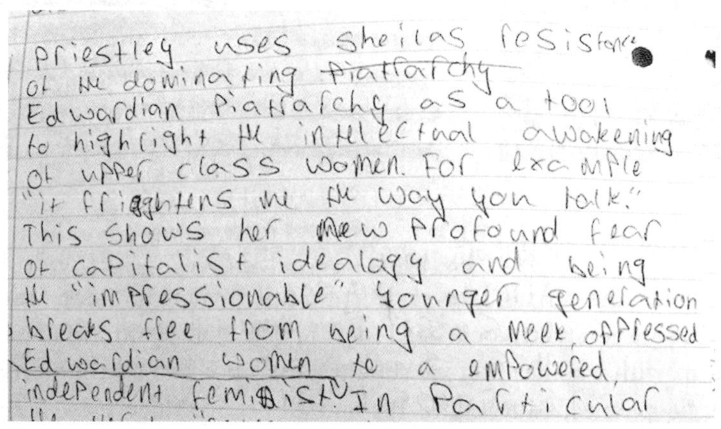

priestley uses sheilas resistance
of the dominating ~~piatrarchy~~
Edwardian piatrarchy as a tool
to highlight the intellectual awakening
of upper class women. For example
"it frigghtens me the way you talk."
This shows her ~~new~~ profound fear
of capitalist idealogy and being
the "impressionable" younger generation
breaks free from being a meek, oppressed
Edwardian women to a empowered,
independent feminist. In particular

64. Mortimore, K. (2020) 'Literacy – providing the equipment to climb the curriculum mountain'. Retrieved from: https://kathrinemortimore.wordpress.com/2020/02/22/literacy-providing-the-equipment-to-climb-the-curriculum-mountain (accessed 19.09.20)
65. Education Endowment Foundation. (2019) *Improving Literacy in Secondary Schools: guidance report*. Retrieved from: https://educationendowmentfoundation.org.uk/tools/guidance-reports/improving-literacy-in-secondary-schools (accessed 19.09.20)

The Word of the Week/Day concept is nothing new and it can often fail to have an impact. This reason for this, as is often the case, is ineffective implementation. To ensure that explicit vocabulary teaching is embedded at Torquay Academy and has the desired outcome, this is how we have implemented Word of the Week:

- Words of the Week are mapped systematically alongside the curriculum. It is not words that allow students to unlock factual information that are necessarily important, such as 'suffragette' when teaching *An Inspector Calls*. It is more the vocabulary that allows young people to express ideas surrounding the text. So, rather than 'suffragette', it is more useful for students to understand 'emancipation'. This term can also be more universally applied to other texts.
- Vocabulary is interwoven with the teaching in that particular week and revisited regularly, with frequent opportunities to practise using the word. So, along with the initial 15-minute explicit teaching episode at the start of the week, the word also appears repeatedly in the curriculum for that week.
- New vocabulary is applied backwards as well as forwards, which can bring new understanding to a previously taught text/concept. Five-a-day retrieval questions balance recap with new knowledge.
- Students have materials they can access independently in order to refer to key terms and recap their learning. Our homework is based on knowledge organisers, which contain all the necessary information, but as these are produced each cycle they can be perceived as 'done' once the cycle is over. The idea of the TA Dictionary is to keep the learning relevant throughout students' school careers.
- Practice is oral as well as written. Some carefully targeted cold-calling helps to build young people's confidence in showing off their mastery of a new word; the impact of this feeling of 'cleverness' in front of the class cannot be underestimated. By the time they reach Year 11 and have used and revisited the word 'emasculation' repeatedly, students feel they have something genuinely intelligent to say about Lady Macbeth – and they are right to feel that way.

Alongside other strategies, Word of the Week has resulted in steep improvement in student progress in English. Explicit vocabulary instruction has therefore not been a very difficult 'sell' to the rest of the school. Most subjects had a good handle on their key vocabulary already, particularly with the introduction of knowledge organisers in 2015. Some had already gone down the Word of the Week route. Others were making a much more conscious effort to explicitly teach vocabulary. Others still were already systematically teaching vocabulary very effectively, because that is what great teachers with access to well-structured curricula do.

Producing the dictionary

The different stages of the project were as follows:

1. Identify the vocabulary terms for each subject, cycle and year group.
2. Come up with an appropriate layout/format/organisation.
3. Write the pages in collaboration with department areas to ensure accuracy.
4. Produce an index of all terms and where they can be found.
5. Work with suppliers to produce final design/front cover/binding.
6. Decide on practical uses for the dictionary in the classroom.

1. Identifying the terms

The fact that knowledge organisers were already in place made identifying the key words much easier. Many subjects had designed a 'key vocabulary' section; if not, it was easy to pull out the words from the knowledge organisers themselves.

Different subject areas had varying levels of involvement in producing the pages. English and MFL wrote their own pages. John Mellitt's science team came up with a 'science word bank' that cut across year groups and cycles and contained what they felt were the essential concepts. They provided the terms and the 'vocabulary team' (a small team of dedicated English teachers) wrote up the definitions, which were checked with the subject specialists. For a small number of subjects, I found their knowledge organisers, pulled out what looked to be the key terms and ran the pages past the department when they were drafted.

2. Coming up with the layout/format/organisation

The first draft of the dictionary was organised into year groups and cycles, the idea being that students could make links between their learning in different curriculum areas. However, feedback from students indicated that they would prefer words from each subject to be grouped together. This is because they tend to use the dictionary when they are writing about a topic, so they find it useful to be able to access either prior learning or more advanced learning to support their understanding and expression. We decided the second draft would also have a small tab on the sides of the pages to make sections easier to find.

In the first draft, the English pages looked like this:

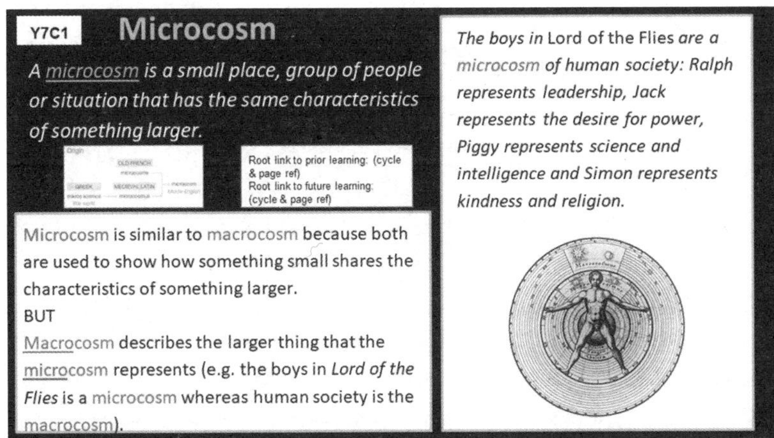

This page is essentially a snapshot of the explicit vocabulary teaching slides students had encountered. Initially, the plan was to include the box that connects the root of the word to prior learning. However, many, many, *many* hours of writing dictionary pages later, it became obvious that it was not going to be possible to produce pages like this alongside teaching commitments. Nevertheless, the index still allows students to see at a glance where the same word comes up across disciplines. Often, seeing that word in the various contexts with its subtly different meanings, as in the first image below, helps to cement their understanding.

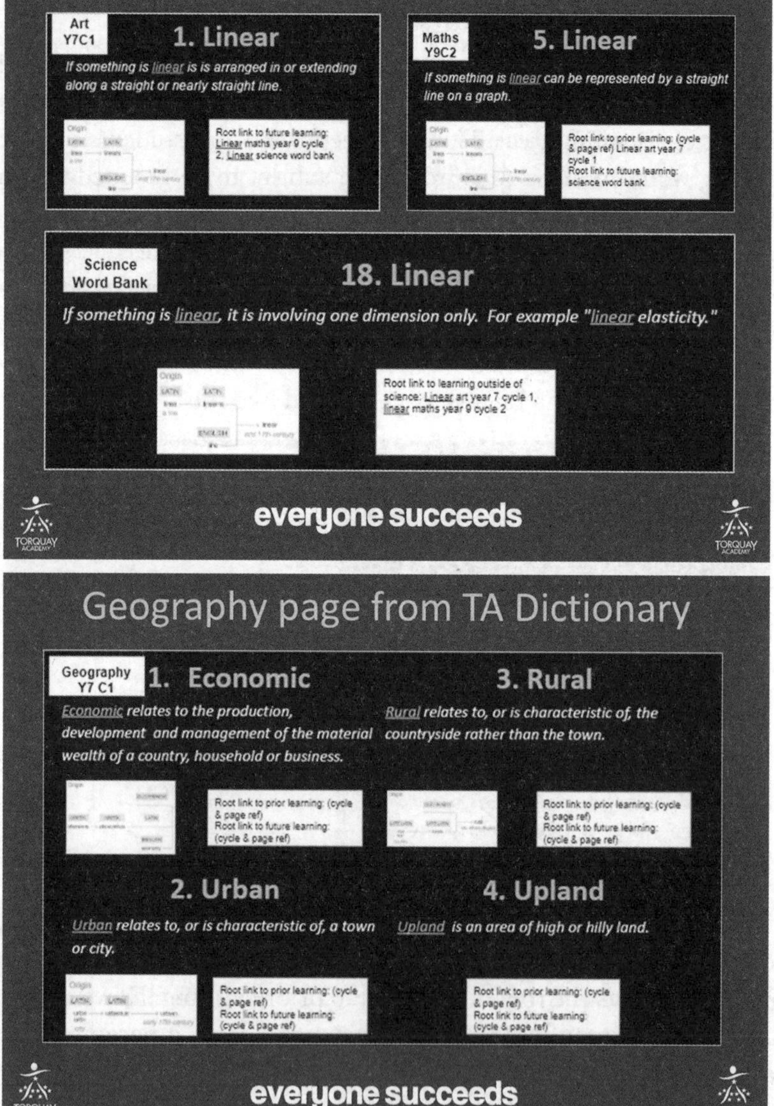

It also became apparent that we were not going to have enough space for all pages to mimic the design of the English pages. The second image opposite is a sample geography page from the dictionary's second draft.

One of the key aspects of the dictionary was the etymology of the words. It is important that students have strategies to work out what unfamiliar words mean. A lack of such strategies is the central reason why GL Assessment[66] found it was far more challenging for students to access English language papers and those in a variety of other subjects than to access the English literature paper. In literature, students are mainly given material they have encountered before, with a teacher to guide them. It is also not essential for them to understand all the words on the paper – they just need enough of a springboard to launch their analysis of a character or theme.

We took screenshots of the words' etymology from Google, but in the printed first draft these screenshots were of variable quality. We also felt that the etymology was not foregrounded enough. Later, alongside dictionary production, our amazing SEN department (especially Carol Rowan) began producing displays of each of the key words:

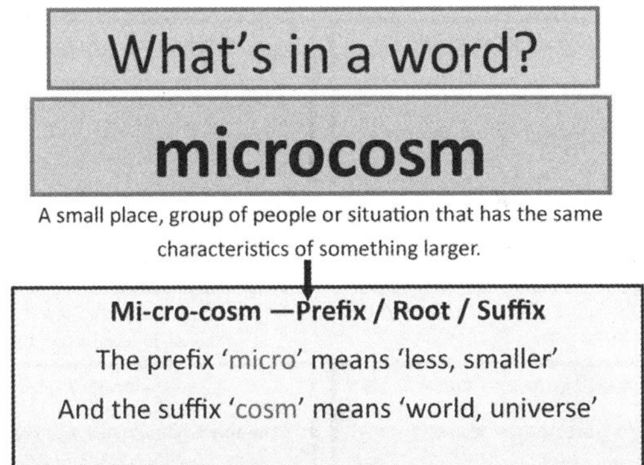

I was a bit slow on the uptake, but I realised that our next draft of the dictionary needed to incorporate all this amazing work. We had a page of common roots/prefixes/suffixes in the first draft, but the second draft covers this information more comprehensively, as you can see overleaf.

66. GL Assessment. (2020) *Read All About It: why reading is key to GCSE success*. Retrieved from: www.gl-assessment.co.uk/whyreading (accessed 19.09.20)

constant

A number expressing a relation or property which remains the same in all circumstances.

Con-stant — Prefix / Root / Suffix

The prefix 'con' means 'together'

The root 'sta' means 'to stand'

And the suffix 'ant' means 'ing'

direction

A course along which something or someone moves.

Di-rec-tion — Prefix / Root / Suffix

The prefix 'di' means 'down'

The root 're' from the Latin 'regere' meaning 'straight'

And the suffix 'tion' means 'act or process of'

discovery

Being the first to find or observe a place, substance or phenomenon .

Dis-cov-er-y — Prefix / Root / Suffix

The prefix 'dis' means 'not'

The root 'cover' from the Latin 'cooperire' meaning 'covered'

And the suffix 'y' means 'characterized by'

effect

A physical phenomenon, often named after it's discoverer.

Ef-fect — Prefix / Root / Suffix

The prefix 'ef' means 'out/away'

And the suffix 'fect' from the Latin 'facere' meaning 'to make'

equation

A symbolic representation of the changes which occur in a chemical reaction.

E-qua-tion — Prefix / Root / Suffix

The prefix 'equa' means 'equal'

And the suffix 'tion' means 'act or process of'

equivalent

Refers to mess of a particular substance that can combine with or displace one gram of hydrogen or eight grams of oxygen.

E-quiv-a-lent — Prefix / Root / Suffix

The prefix 'equ' means 'equal'

The root 'val' means 'value'

And the suffix 'ent' means 'ing'

factor

A gene that determines a hereditary characteristic .

Fac-tor — Prefix / Root / Suffix

The prefix 'fact' means 'done'

And the suffix 'or' means 'one who'

flows

A liquid , gas or electricity flows if it moves steadily and continuously in a current or stream.

Flow-s —Prefix / Root / Suffix

The prefix 'flow' from the Old English 'flod' meaning 'flood'

And the suffix 's' means 'plural'

3. Writing the pages and ensuring accuracy

As I explained earlier, English and MFL wrote their own pages and a small team of English teachers, including Natalie Jones, wrote the pages for all the other subjects in their own time. This is the part that schools need to balance carefully if they undertake a similar project. A passionate belief that our young people deserved this dictionary drove this small team to voluntarily give up their time to produce it. Staff should not be expected to produce pages for their department areas unless they are happy to do so voluntarily, or are given adequate time to get the work done during the school day. Our pages were created in Google Slides and shared with the relevant departments to check before they were sent to the printers.

4. Producing an index

This was one of the hardest parts of the book to write. All the terms had been saved in a central Google document divided into different boxes for each subject, year group and cycle. The terms now needed to be alphabetised, with the subject, cycle and year group recorded next to each one. The fact that this was really interesting work kept me from going bananas as words or the order in which they were taught changed. We had several Inset days for curriculum improvement at the end of 2019, which inevitably led to wholesale changes to the pages for a number of subjects. I completely understood the need for changes and it was great that the staff wanted to get the dictionary right, but it made my work very tricky. So, lesson learned: creating the index must always be the very, very last job!

What made the index so interesting was finding the commonalities across subjects. It was unsurprising how many terms taught in RS and history were also taught in English, but it was really useful to pinpoint exactly which concepts were taught when. I am keen for us to actually recycle resources to make accessing prior knowledge even more straightforward, and the Inset we ran in September 2019 suggested the dictionary might also be useful as a resource for teachers when planning lessons. In the past, there has been a tendency to keep resources locked away – a sense that if they are 'done' then that's it, their usefulness is exhausted. I think the opposite is true, not for entire lessons, but for key slides/extracts/worksheets. Linking prior learning to new learning in a way that builds confidence and familiarity can only be a good thing, particularly for our disadvantaged students.

5. Working with suppliers

We have built up a relationship with a supplier that creates all our exercise books and revision materials. The dictionary was an extension to this, but it turned out to be quite complex. There were different files that needed organising in a very specific way and communication was not always straightforward. The number of pages also exceeded the usual maximum for the type of binding we use, so the dictionary needed to be sent to a separate binding company. It is fair to say that this was the bumpiest part of the road, but again, we learned lots of lessons for next time.

6. Deciding on practical uses in the classroom

We are still in the early days of implementation and will adapt how we use the dictionary as we receive more feedback from students and teachers. Here is how we currently envisage the dictionary being used in the classroom:

- To support the delivery of Word of the Week (students can look up the word or refer to the dictionary if the teacher is going too quickly for them or they arrive late to the lesson).
- During five-a-day retrieval practice. Much of this retrieval practice revisits vocabulary that may have been taught years earlier, so the dictionary provides a useful reference point for 'no opt out'.
- During 'superteaching' (for us, this is the week after assessment week) to support redrafting. Similarly, within 'purple pen' lessons once students have received formative feedback on mid-point assessments.
- When essay planning and preparing for assessments.
- In reading lessons (once a fortnight for KS3) as part of the 'do now' task (which is creative writing after reading an extract).
- During homework, alongside knowledge organisers/assessment preparation, or alongside reading journals (students complete one Frayer model a week).
- To support the use of Frayer models, pictured opposite (some subject departments were already using these).

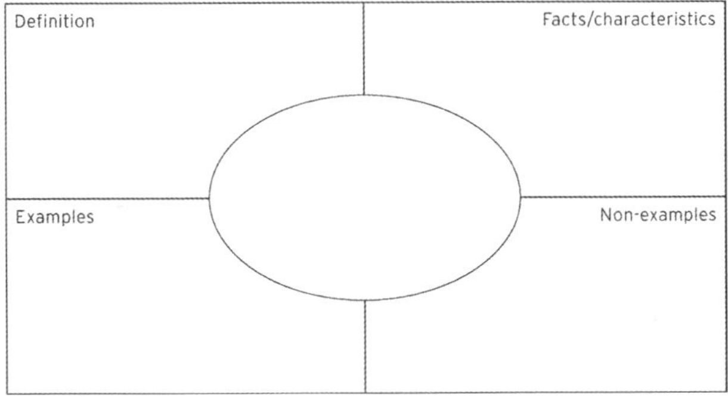

TA Dictionary word bank

On the following pages is the list of almost 1,700 key terms that appears in the TA Dictionary. If you wish to create your own dictionary, we have made a template available here: https://tinyurl.com/y5lsm44k

Word	Subject
abstract	Art Y7 C2
action planning	Art Y8 C4
analogous	Art Y7 C3
annotation	Art Y8 C2, C4
clashing	Art Y8 C2
complementary	Art Y7 C3
composition	Art Y7 C1
contemporary	Art Y7 C3
contour	Art Y7 C2
contrast	Art Y8 C1
creativity	Art Y8 C2
density	Art Y7 C3
depth (of mark)	Art Y8 C1
emphasis	Art Y7 C4
evaluation	Art Y7 C4, Y8 C4
expressionism	Art Y8 C3
expressive	Art Y8 C2
focal point	Art Y7 C1
fragmented	Art Y8 C3
genre	Art Y7 C4
graduated	Art Y8 C1
harmonious	Art Y8 C2
hue	Art Y7 C3
interpretation	Art Y8 C3
linear	Art Y7 C1
media	Art Y8 C1
medium	Art Y7 C1
mirror image	Art Y8 C3
mixed media	Art Y8 C2
monochromatic	Art Y7 C2
negative	Art Y7 C2, C4
perspective	Art Y7 C1
positive	Art Y7 C2, C4
primary	Art Y7 C3
proportion	Art Y7 C2
recording	Art Y8 C4
reflection	Art Y7 C4
repetition	Art Y7 C4
research	Art Y8 C3
secondary	Art Y7 C3
shade	Art Y7 C1
symbolism	Art Y7 C3
symmetrical	Art Y8 C3
tessellation	Art Y7 C4
texture	Art Y7 C2
three-dimensional	Art Y8 C2
tonal (values)	Art Y8 C1
tone	Art Y7 C1
value	Art Y7 C2
visual (element)	Art Y8 C1
acronym	Automotive word bank
alternator	Automotive word bank
bump	Automotive word bank
camber	Automotive word bank
camshaft	Automotive word bank
caster	Automotive word bank
combustion chamber	Automotive word bank
compression ignition	Automotive word bank

Word	Subject
COSHH	Automotive word bank
crankshaft	Automotive word bank
current	Automotive word bank
cylinder head	Automotive word bank
dive	Automotive word bank
ECU	Automotive word bank
employee	Automotive word bank
employer	Automotive word bank
engine block	Automotive word bank
EPA	Automotive word bank
exhaust pipe	Automotive word bank
fuel injector	Automotive word bank
gasoline	Automotive word bank
HASAWA	Automotive word bank
hemispherical chamber	Automotive word bank
hydraulic	Automotive word bank
hygroscopic	Automotive word bank
independent front suspension	Automotive word bank
independent rear suspension	Automotive word bank
modulator	Automotive word bank
oversteer	Automotive word bank
piston	Automotive word bank
pitch	Automotive word bank
PPE	Automotive word bank
PUWER	Automotive word bank
radiator	Automotive word bank
range	Automotive word bank
rebound	Automotive word bank
resistance	Automotive word bank
RIDDOR	Automotive word bank
roll spark plug	Automotive word bank
solvent	Automotive word bank
squat	Automotive word bank
starter motor	Automotive word bank
SWL	Automotive word bank
terminal	Automotive word bank
timing belt	Automotive word bank
understeer	Automotive word bank
valves	Automotive word bank
voltage	Automotive word bank
yaw	Automotive word bank
advantage	Business Y10 C4
aesthetics	Business Y10 C4
asset	Business Y11 C4
automation	Business Y10 C4
autonomy	Business Y11 C3
average	Business Y11 C1, C2
bankruptcy	Business Y9 C2
biased	Business Y9 C2
calculation	Business Y11 C4
capital	Business Y10 C3
centralised	Business Y11 C2
characteristics	Business Y10 C3
communication	Business Y11 C2
company	Business Y10 C1
compliance	Business Y10 C2
conflict	Business Y10 C2

Word	Subject
consumables	Business Y9 C2
convenience	Business Y9 C3
culture	Business Y11 C1
curriculum vitae	Business Y11 C2
deed	Business Y9 C3
demographic	Business Y9 C1
differentiation	Business Y9 C4
director	Business Y10 C1
discrimination	Business Y10 C2
dynamic	Business Y9 C1
economy	Business Y9 C1
efficiency	Business Y10 C4
empower	Business Y11 C3
engagement	Business Y11 C1
enrichment	Business Y11 C3
entrepreneur	Business Y9 C1
environmental	Business Y10 C4
ethics	Business Y10 C1
exchange	Business Y10 C3, Y11 C4
export	Business Y10 C2
external	Business Y11 C4
flotation	Business Y10 C3
footfall	Business Y9 C3
franchise	Business Y9 C3
freelance	Business Y11 C2
function	Business Y10 C4
gig economy	Business Y11 C2
globalisation	Business Y10 C3
hierarchical	Business Y11 C2
import	Business Y10 C2
incorporated	Business Y9 C3
induction	Business Y10 C2
inertia	Business Y9 C4
inflation	Business Y11 C4
innovation	Business Y10 C3
insolvent	Business Y9 C2
internal	Business Y11 C4
intuition	Business Y9 C1
investment	Business Y9 C1
labour	Business Y9 C3
legislation	Business Y10 C2
liability	Business Y9 C3
logistics	Business Y11 C1
loyalty	Business Y9 C4
majority	Business Y10 C1
market	Business Y9 C4
mentor	Business Y11 C3
merger	Business Y10 C3
minority	Business Y10 C1
motivation	Business Y11 C1
multinational	Business Y10 C1
obsolete	Business Y9 C1
organisation	Business Y11 C2
partnership	Business Y9 C4
percentage	Business Y11 C1, C2
performance	Business Y11 C3
procurement	Business Y11 C1

Word	Subject
productivity	Business Y10 C4
profit	Business Y10 C1
qualitative	Business Y9 C1
quantitative	Business Y9 C2
recession	Business Y9 C4
recruitment	Business Y11 C2
remuneration	Business Y11 C3
research	Business Y9 C4
retained	Business Y11 C4
retention	Business Y11 C3
revenue	Business Y9 C4
rotation	Business Y11 C3
segmentation	Business Y9 C2
shareholder	Business Y10 C1
stakeholder	Business Y10 C2
sustainability	Business Y10 C4
tariff	Business Y10 C3
topography	Business Y9 C3
unemployment	Business Y11 C4
venture	Business Y9 C2
viable	Business Y9 C1
warranty	Business Y11 C1
abrasive paper	Construction word bank
aesthetics	Construction word bank
affordable housing	Construction word bank
annotations	Construction word bank
building services	Construction word bank
built environment	Construction word bank
buy-to-let	Construction word bank
carbon footprint	Construction word bank
construct	Construction Word Bank
corner half-lap joint	Construction word bank
dimensions	Construction word bank
dovetail halving joint	Construction word bank
drawing boards	Construction word bank
elevations	Construction word bank
feasibility tendering	Construction word bank
FSC	Construction word bank
glue	Construction word bank
grey water	Construction word bank
hatchings	Construction word bank
imperfections	Construction word bank
infrastructure	Construction word bank
lines	Construction word bank
local planning	Construction word bank
location drawing	Construction word bank
manually	Construction word bank
MDF	Construction word bank
mortise and tenon joint	Construction word bank
orientation	Construction word bank
outline planning permission	Construction word bank
photovoltaic	Construction word bank
plans	Construction word bank
plywood	Construction word bank
porosity	Construction word bank
PPE	Construction word bank
projection methods	Construction word bank

Word	Subject
protractor	Construction word bank
PVA	Construction word bank
sections	Construction word bank
set square	Construction word bank
stencil	Construction word bank
sustainability	Construction word bank
tee-bridle joint	Construction word bank
wood composite	Construction word bank
wood/timber	Construction word bank
antenatal	CPLD Y9 C2
Apgar score	CPLD Y9 C2
bed guard	CPLD Y10 C4, Y11 C4
breast milk	CPLD Y10 C1
breathing difficulties	CPLD Y10 C3, Y11 C4
BSI safety mark	CPLD Y10 C3, Y11 C4
CE symbol	CPLD Y10 C3, Y11 C3
co-operative play	CPLD Y11 C1, C2
conception	CPLD Y9 C1
contraception	CPLD Y9 C1
creative play	CPLD Y11 C2, C2
cutlery	CPLD Y10 C4, Y11 C4
development	CPLD Y9 C3
developmental norms	CPLD Y9 C3
diarrhoea	CPLD Y10 C3, Y11 C3
duvet	CPLD Y10 C4, Y11 C4
eat well plate	CPLD Y10 C1
embryo	CPLD Y9 C1
evaluation	CPLD Y10 C2
fatty acids	CPLD Y10 C1
feeding equipment	CPLD Y10 C4, Y11 C4
feeding solution	CPLD Y10 C2
fibre	CPLD Y10 C1
fitting	CPLD Y10 C3, Y11 C3
foetus	CPLD Y9 C1
footwear	CPLD Y10 C4, Y11 C4
formula milk	CPLD Y10 C1
genetic counselling	CPLD Y9 C1
hazard	CPLD Y10 C3, Y11 C3
health visitor	CPLD Y9 C2
high temperature	CPLD Y10 C3, Y11 C3
holistic development	CPLD Y9 C3
holistic play	CPLD Y11 C1, Y11 C2
implantation	CPLD Y9 C1
independence	CPLD Y9 C4
intellectual development	CPLD Y9 C3
macronutrients	CPLD Y9 C4
main food groups	CPLD Y10 C2
manipulative play	CPLD Y11 C1, Y11 C2
micronutrients	CPLD Y9 C4
midwife	CPLD Y9 C2
milestones	CPLD Y9 C3
minerals	CPLD Y9 C4
motor skills	CPLD Y9 C3
nutritional analysis	CPLD Y10 C2
observation	CPLD Y11 C1, C2
obstetrician	CPLD Y9 C2
physical development	CPLD Y9 C3

Word	Subject
physical play	CPLD Y11 C1, C2
post-natal	CPLD Y9 C2
pre-conception health	CPLD Y9 C1
prebiotics	CPLD Y10 C1
premature	CPLD Y9 C2
reflexes	CPLD Y9 C3
role model	CPLD Y9 C1
role play	CPLD Y11 C1, C2
safety strategies	CPLD Y10 C3, C4, Y11 C3, C4
self-esteem	CPLD Y9 C4
sleeping equipment	CPLD Y10 C4, Y11 C4
social development	CPLD Y9 C4
soya milk	CPLD Y10 C1
stroller/buggy	CPLD Y10 C4, Y11 C4
symptoms of illness	CPLD Y10 C3, Y11 C3
trainer cups	CPLD Y10 C4, Y11 C4
travel equipment	CPLD Y10 C4, Y11 C4
unresponsive	CPLD Y10 C3, Y11 C4
vitamin	CPLD Y9 C4, Y10 C1
vomiting	CPLD Y10 C3, Y11 C3
water	CPLD Y10 C1
weaning bibs	CPLD Y10 C4, Y11 C4
weaning stage	CPLD Y9 C4
abrasive	D&T Y7 C1
acrid	D&T Y7 C4
aerodynamics	D&T Y8 C3
aroma	D&T Y7 C4
bradawl	D&T Y7 C1
brittle	D&T Y7 C4
carbohydrate	D&T Y8 C2
composite	D&T Y8 C1
compression	D&T Y8 C3
coniferous	D&T Y7 C1
contamination	D&T Y7 C4
deciduous	D&T Y7 C1
designer	D&T Y7 C2
detritivore	D&T Y7 C1
endurance	D&T Y8 C3
fats	D&T Y8 C2
felling	D&T Y7 C1
filament	D&T Y7 C2
firewall	D&T Y7 C3
friction	D&T Y8 C3
hazard	D&T Y7 C4
herbivore	D&T Y7 C1
hydration	D&T Y8 C4
isometric	D&T Y7 C2
kevlar	D&T Y8 C1
kneading	D&T Y8 C4
laser	D&T Y8 C1
macronutrients	D&T Y8 C2
maker	D&T Y7 C2
manufacture	D&T Y8 C1
micronutrients	D&T Y8 C2
orthographic	D&T Y7 C2
phishing	D&T Y7 C3
porous/nonporous	D&T Y8 C1

Word	Subject
protein	D&T Y8 C2
prototype	D&T Y7 C3
prototyping	D&T Y7 C2
proving	D&T Y8 C4
raising agent	D&T Y8 C4
robot	D&T Y7 C3
spyware	D&T Y7 C3
texture	D&T Y7 C4
torsion	D&T Y8 C3
triangulation	D&T Y8 C3
typography	D&T Y7 C3
ventilation	D&T Y8 C1
whole grain	D&T Y8 C4
wholemeal	D&T Y8 C4
abhorrent	English Y8 C3
adversary	English Y7 C3
adversity	English Y8 C2
agency	English Y10 C3
alienation	English Y9 C2
allegorical	English Y7 C2
altruistic	English Y10 C2
ambiguous	English Y8 C1
anguish	English Y8 C2
animosity	English Y7 C3
antithesis	English Y11 C3
anxiety	English Y8 C1
apathy	English Y7 C2
archetypal	English Y7 C2
atrocity	English Y9 C4
avarice	English Y10 C2
benevolence	English Y11 C3
cacophony	English Y9 C2
charismatic	English Y7 C1
coercion	English Y7 C1
colonialism	English Y9 C3
commodification	English Y10 C4
condemned	English Y8 C2
corrosive	English Y9 C4
corruption	English Y9 C1
courteous	English Y7 C2
critique	English Y8 C2
culture	English Y9 C3
cynical	English Y8 C4
damnation	English Y11 C2
denounce	English Y7 C4
despondency	English Y9 C2
despondent	English Y11 C2
destitute	English Y8 C3
destitution	English Y9 C4
dictatorial	English Y8 C2
didactic	English Y10 C1
discrimination	English Y9 C3
disempowering	English Y10 C4
disintegration	English Y10 C4
duality	English Y8 C1
eccentric	English Y8 C2
egalitarian	English Y9 C1

Word	Subject
ego	English Y11 C1
elitism	English Y9 C1
emancipation	English Y10 C4, Y11 C1
emasculate	English Y10 C3
empathy	English Y8 C3
entrapment	English Y8 C1
ephemeral	English Y10 C2
epidemic	English Y9 C4
epiphany	English Y7 C4
ethnicity	English Y9 C3
euphoria	English Y9 C2, Y11 C4
exploitation	English Y10 C1, Y11 C1
exultation	English Y9 C2
façade	English Y10 C1
fatalism	English Y7 C3
futile	English Y10 C3
grotesque	English Y8 C1
harrowing	English Y8 C3
hubristic	English Y10 C4
hypocrisy	English Y10 C1
idealise	English Y11 C2
idealistic	English Y8 C4
ideology	English Y9 C1
idolatry	English Y7 C3
idyllic	English Y7 C4
ignorance	English Y7 C2
illegitimate	English Y10 C3
immoral	English Y7 C4, Y11 C1
impoverished	English Y8 C2
ineffable	English Y10 C4
inertia	English Y11 C2
infatuation	English Y7 C3
insidious	English Y11 C2
insincerity	English Y7 C2
institution	English Y9 C3
jingoism	English Y8 C3
mammon	English Y10 C2
manifestation	English Y11 C3
marginalisation	English Y8 C4
melancholic	English Y8 C4
microcosm	English Y7 C1
migrant	English Y8 C4
misanthropic	English Y10 C2
myopic	English Y10 C1
naivety	English Y9 C1
narcissism	English Y9 C2
negligent	English Y11 C3
neurotic	English Y10 C3
nihilistic	English Y10 C3
nostalgia	English Y9 C2
objectification	English Y9 C3
ominous	English Y8 C2
ostracise	English Y7 C1
pantheism	English Y7 C4
paragon	English Y9 C4
paramount	English Y9 C4
parody	English Y11 C1

Word	Subject
pathos	English Y9 C4
patriarchy	English Y10 C1
patriotism	English Y10 C4
perceptive	English Y11 C2
persecution	English Y8 C3
philanthropic	English Y10 C2
polemic	English Y9 C4
predestination	English Y10 C3
prejudice	English Y9 C2
primitive	English Y7 C1
profound	English Y11 C1
quixotic	English Y7 C2
reconciliation	English Y7 C3
redemption	English Y10 C2
regime	English Y9 C1
repentance	English Y10 C2
repercussion	English Y8 C3
repression	English Y8 C1
repugnant	English Y11 C2
retribution	English Y7 C3
revelation	English Y10 C1
sadistic	English Y7 C1
sanctity	English Y11 C3
savagery	English Y7 C1
segregation	English Y9 C3
sentimental	English Y7 C4
sinister	English Y9 C2
solace	English Y7 C4, Y11 C4
sombre	English Y11 C3
stance	English Y11 C1
subjugation	English Y8 C4
sublime	English Y7 C4
subversive	English Y10 C3
superficial	English Y9 C1
suppression	English Y10 C1
tangible	English Y11 C3
tragedy	English Y8 C4
trajectory	English Y11 C4
transcendental	English Y11 C1
transgression	English Y8 C1
transitory	English Y8 C4
traumatising	English Y8 C3
treachery	English Y9 C1
turmoil	English Y11 C3
tyranny	English Y7 C1
uncanny	English Y8 C1
vacuous	English Y11 C2
visceral	English Y10 C4
woeful	English Y7 C3
allergy	Food Y10 C4
blending	Food Y9 C4
braising	Food Y9 C4
carbohydrate	Food Y10 C1, Y11 C1
clostridium perfringens	Food Y9 C1
contingency	Food Y10 C3, Y11 C2
COSHH	Food Y10 C2, Y11 C3
customer	Food Y10 C4

Word	Subject
demographic	Food Y11 C4
dovetailing	Food Y10 C3, Y11 C2
EHO	Food Y10 C2, Y11 C3
environmental	Food Y11 C4
equality	Food Y10 C4
escherichia coli	Food Y9 C1
fat	Food Y9 C3
flour	Food Y9 C3
food provenance	Food Y10 C3, Y11 C2
function	Food Y10 C1, Y11 C1
HACCP	Food Y10 C2, Y11 C3
HASAWA	Food Y10 C2, Y11 C3
hazard	Food Y9 C1
HBV/LBV	Food Y10 C1, Y11 C1
intolerance	Food Y9 C1, Y10 C4
market research	Food Y10 C4
menu	Food Y10 C3, Y11 C2
MHOR	Food Y10 C2, Y11 C3
microbe	Food Y9 C1
monitoring	Food Y9 C2
organoleptic	Food Y9 C4
pathogen	Food Y9 C2
peeling	Food Y9 C2
poaching	Food Y9 C4
political	Food Y11 C4
PPE	Food Y10 C2, Y11 C3
protein	Food Y11 C1, Y10 C1
psychographic	Food Y11 C4
purpose	Food Y9 C4
RIDDOR	Food Y10 C2, Y11 C3
risk assessment	Food Y10 C2, Y11 C3
salmonella	Food Y9 C1
sautéing	Food Y9 C4
seasonality	Food Y10 C3, Y11 C2
segment	Food Y9 C4
sieving	Food Y9 C4
slicing	Food Y9 C2
socioeconomic	Food Y11 C4
staphylococcus aureus	Food Y9 C1
structure	Food Y9 C3
sustainability	Food Y10 C3, Y11 C2
taste	Food Y9 C3
technological	Food Y11 C4
temperature	Food Y9 C2, C3
timings	Food Y10 C3, Y11 C2
toxin	Food Y9 C1
trimming	Food Y9 C2
utility	Food Y11 C4
variable	Food Y11 C4
vitamin	Food Y10 C1, Y11 C1
waste	Food Y9 C2
zesting	Food Y9 C4
abiotic	Geo Y7 C3
abrasion	Geo Y8 C3, Y10 C2
adaptation	Geo Y10 C3
altitude	Geo Y7 C4
anemometer	Geo Y7 C4

Word	Subject
anticyclone	Geo Y9 C2
attrition	Geo Y8 C3, Y10 C1
biodiversity	Geo Y7 C3
biomass	Geo Y7 C2
biome	Geo Y7 C3
biotic	Geo Y7 C3
brownfield site	Geo Y9 C4
calorie	Geo Y10 C4
camouflage	Geo Y10 C3
climate	Geo Y7 C4
conservative	Geo Y8 C1, Y9 C1
constructive plate	Geo Y8 C1, Y9 C1
continental plate	Geo Y8 C1, Y9 C1
continentality	Geo Y7 C4
convection	Geo Y9 C2
coriolis effect	Geo Y9 C2
corrosion	Geo Y8 C3
cross profile	Geo Y10 C2
debit crisis	Geo Y11 C3
decomposer	Geo Y7 C3
deficit	Geo Y10 C4, Y11 C1
deforestation	Geo Y10 C3
degradation	Geo Y10 C3
demand	Geo Y10 C4
democracy	Geo Y11 C3
demographic	Geo Y11 C2
demographics	Geo Y8 C4
dense	Geo Y8 C4
dense population	Geo Y9 C4
density	Geo Y8 C4
deposition	Geo Y8 C3, Y10 C1
depression	Geo Y9 C2
deprivation	Geo Y9 C4
desalination	Geo Y10 C4
destructive plate	Geo Y8 C1, Y9 C1
development	Geo Y8 C2, Y11 C2
economic	Geo Y7 C1
economy	Geo Y8 C2, Y9 C3
employment	Geo Y8 C4
environment	Geo Y7 C3
estuary	Geo Y10 C2
evapotranspiration	Geo Y10 C3
exponential	Geo Y8 C4
fluvial	Geo Y8 C3
fluvial processes	Geo Y10 C2
gentrification	Geo Y9 C3, C4
geothermal	Geo Y7 C2
glaciated	Geo Y7 C1
globalisation	Geo Y11 C3
greenfield site	Geo Y9 C4
hydraulic	Geo Y10 C1
hydroelectric	Geo Y7 C2
hydrograph	Geo Y8 C3
industry	Geo Y8 C2
inequality	Geo Y10 C4
infrastructure	Geo Y8 C2
lateral erosion	Geo Y10 C2

Word	Subject
latitude	Geo Y7 C4
life expectancy	Geo Y8 C4
long profile	Geo Y10 C2
lowland	Geo Y7 C1
malnourishment	Geo Y10 C4
maritime	Geo Y7 C4
meander	Geo Y10 C2
mechanical	Geo Y10 C1
microclimate	Geo Y9 C2
migration	Geo Y8 C2, Y11 C3
mortality	Geo Y11 C2
multiplier effect	Geo Y11 C2
nuclear power	Geo Y7 C2
oceanic plate	Geo Y8 C1, Y9 C1
plate margin	Geo Y8 C1, Y9 C1
pollution	Geo Y9 C3
population	Geo Y9 C3, Y11 C3
poverty	Geo Y8 C2
precipitation	Geo Y9 C2
producer	Geo Y7 C3
qualitative	Geo Y11 C1
quantitative	Geo Y11 C1
radiation	Geo Y7 C2
remittances	Geo Y11 C2
renewable	Geo Y7 C2
river discharge	Geo Y10 C2
rural	Geo Y7 C1
sanitation	Geo Y9 C3
scarcity	Geo Y10 C4, Y11 C1
selective logging	Geo Y10 C3
settlement	Geo Y10 C3
sparse	Geo Y8 C4
sparse population	Geo Y9 C4
stratified	Geo Y11 C1
stress	Geo Y11 C1
subsistence	Geo Y10 C3
surplus	Geo Y10 C4, Y11 C1
sustainable	Geo Y11 C2
systematic	Geo Y11 C1
tectonic	Geo Y8 C1, Y9 C1
thermal expansion	Geo Y9 C2
transnational	Geo Y11 C2
transportation	Geo Y8 C3, Y10 C1
upland	Geo Y7 C1
urban	Geo Y7 C1, Y9 C4
urban regeneration	Geo Y9 C4
urbanisation	Geo Y8 C2, Y9 C3, Y11 C3
vertical erosion	Geo Y10 C2
weather	Geo Y7 C4
weathering	Geo Y10 C1
abstract thinking	H&Sc Y9 C2
ADHD	H&Sc Y9 C3
advocates	H&Sc Y10 C1
AED	H&Sc Y11 C2
airway	H&Sc Y11 C1
autism	H&Sc Y9 C2
bereavement	H&Sc Y9 C3

Word	Subject
birth defects	H&Sc Y9 C4
care plan	H&Sc Y10 C1
casualty	H&Sc Y11 C1
cerebral palsy	H&Sc Y9 C2, Y10 C2
cognitive development	H&Sc Y9 C2
conscious	H&Sc Y11 C1
CPR	H&Sc Y11 C2
dementia	H&Sc Y10 C1, C4
disableism	H&Sc Y10 C4
discrimination	H&Sc Y10 C3, C4
diversity	H&Sc Y10 C3
dyslexia	H&Sc Y10 C2
emotional abuse	H&Sc Y10 C2
empathy	H&Sc Y10 C1
empower	H&Sc Y10 C4
equality	H&Sc Y10 C3
fine motor skills	H&Sc Y9 C1
genetics	H&Sc Y9 C4
gross motor skills	H&Sc Y9 C1
halal	H&Sc Y10 C3
harassment	H&Sc Y10 C4
hearing impairment	H&Sc Y10 C3
hospice	H&Sc Y10 C3
hypoglycaemia	H&Sc Y11 C2
insomnia	H&Sc Y10 C2
interpreter	H&Sc Y10 C4
jargon	H&Sc Y10 C1, C4
learning disability	H&Sc Y10 C1
legislation	H&Sc Y10 C4
neural growth	H&Sc Y9 C3
paraphrasing	H&Sc Y10 C2
patronising language	H&Sc Y10 C2
peer group	H&Sc Y9 C1
physical disability	H&Sc Y10 C1
puberty	H&Sc Y9 C1
pulse	H&Sc Y11 C1
radiography assistant	H&Sc Y10 C3
rationale	H&Sc Y11 C2
redress	H&Sc Y10 C4
resilience	H&Sc Y10 C3
risk	H&Sc Y11 C1
severity	H&Sc Y11 C2
sexism	H&Sc Y10 C4
spina bifida	H&Sc Y9 C4
stammers	H&Sc Y10 C2
summarising	H&Sc Y10 C2
translator	H&Sc Y10 C4
transphobia	H&Sc Y10 C4
unconscious	H&Sc Y11 C2
victimisation	H&Sc Y10 C4
vulnerable	H&Sc Y10 C4
abdicate	His Y11 C2
abdication	His Y9 C4
abolition	His Y7 C4
alliance	His Y8 C1
anaesthetic	His Y8 C4
anti-Semitism	His Y8 C2, Y9 C4

Word	Subject
antiseptic	His Y8 C4
appeasement	His Y8 C2
archbishop	His Y7 C2
aristocracy	His Y10 C3
armistice	His Y8 C1
Aryan	His Y8 C2
assassinate	His Y8 C1
assassinated	His Y8 C3
auction	His Y7 C4
bailey	His Y10 C2
boycott	His Y8 C3
burh	His Y7 C1
campaign	His Y8 C3
capitalism	His Y11 C1
castellan	His Y10 C2, C3
Catholicism	His Y7 C3
censorship	His Y10 C1
chancellor	His Y9 C4
change	His Y8 C4
claimant	His Y7 C1
colonialism	His Y11 C1
committee	His Y9 C3
communism	His Y11 C1
conscience	His Y9 C1
conscription	His Y8 C2
constitution	His Y9 C4
continuity	His Y8 C4
control	His Y10 C1
crime	His Y9 C1
cyber	His Y9 C1
dehumanise	His Y7 C4
democracy	His Y11 C1
demonstration	His Y9 C3
desegregation	His Y8 C3
détente	His Y11 C2
deterrent	His Y9 C2
dictatorship	His Y9 C4
discrimination	His Y8 C3, Y9 C1, Y10 C2
doctrine	His Y11 C2
earl	His Y7 C1
economic sanctions	His Y11 C2
emancipation	His Y7 C4
enforcement	His Y9 C2
eugenics	His Y10 C1
extremist	His Y9 C4
federal	His Y10 C4
feudalism	His Y7 C1, Y10 C3
frontier	His Y10 C4
garrison	His Y10 C2
glasnost	His Y11 C2
harrying	His Y10 C2
heir	His Y7 C3
heresy	His Y7 C2
humanitarianism	His Y9 C2
hyperinflation	His Y9 C4
ideology	His Y11 C1
immigration	His Y9 C3

Word	Subject
immunity	His Y8 C4
imperialism	His Y8 C1
indoctrination	His Y10 C1
inevitable	His Y8 C2
inoculate	His Y8 C4
interim	His Y11 C2
isolationism	His Y11 C1
justified	His Y8 C2
kingdom	His Y7 C1
landownership	His Y10 C3
Latin	His Y7 C3
law	His Y9 C1
lawlessness	His Y10 C4
lynching	His Y8 C3
manor	His Y7 C2
media	His Y8 C3
memoir	His Y9 C3
middle passage	His Y7 C4
migration	His Y10 C4
militarism	His Y8 C1
monarch	His Y7 C3
monasteries	His Y10 C2
monastery	His Y7 C2
motte	His Y10 C2
nationalism	His Y8 C1
Norman	His Y7 C1
Normanisation	His Y10 C3
opposition	His Y10 C1
perestroika	His Y11 C2
persecution	His Y10 C1
pilgrimage	His Y7 C2
plantation	His Y7 C4
pope	His Y7 C3
poverty	His Y9 C3
priest	His Y7 C2
prison	His Y9 C2
propaganda	His Y10 C1
Protestantism	His Y7 C3
punishment	His Y9 C2
ranching	His Y10 C4
ratification	His Y11 C2
ration	His Y8 C2
rearmament	His Y10 C1
rebellion	His Y7 C1, Y10 C3
reformation	His Y7 C3, Y9 C2
rehabilitate	His Y9 C2
renaissance	His Y8 C4
reparations	His Y11 C1
reservation	His Y10 C4
resistance	His Y8 C2
retribution	His Y9 C2
sanitation	His Y9 C3
segregationists	His Y8 C3
siege	His Y10 C2
slavery	His Y7 C4
slum	His Y9 C3
stalemate	His Y8 C1

Word	Subject
statute	His Y9 C1
succession	His Y10 C3
surrender	His Y10 C2
tipi	His Y10 C4
trails	His Y10 C4
treason	His Y7 C2, Y9 C1
trench	His Y8 C1
triangular trade	His Y7 C4
uprising	His Y9 C4
vaccinate	His Y8 C4
vagrancy	His Y7 C2, Y9 C1
vassal	His Y10 C3
veto	His Y11 C1
witan	His Y7 C1
workhouse	His Y9 C3
analyse	ICT word bank
analysis	ICT word bank
asset	ICT word bank
audience	ICT word bank
audit	ICT word bank
blending	ICT word bank
concept art	ICT word bank
contrast	ICT word bank
describe	ICT word bank
discuss	ICT word bank
ethnicity	ICT word bank
evaluation	ICT word bank
exporting	ICT word bank
file type	ICT word bank
interactive	ICT word bank
interactivity	ICT word bank
layers	ICT word bank
manipulation	ICT word bank
meaning	ICT word bank
narrative	ICT word bank
principles	ICT word bank
profile	ICT word bank
published	ICT word bank
purpose	ICT word bank
representation	ICT word bank
sans serif	ICT word bank
scaling	ICT word bank
scratch	ICT word bank
sector	ICT word bank
serif	ICT word bank
socioeconomic	ICT word bank
sourcing	ICT word bank
stereotypes	ICT word bank
storyboard	ICT word bank
strength	ICT word bank
subvert	ICT word bank
weaknesses	ICT word bank
wireframe	ICT word bank
adjacent	Maths Y7 C2
alternate	Maths Y8 C2
analyse	Maths Y10 C4
area	Maths Y7 C2, Y9 C4

Word	Subject
ascending	Maths Y7 C1
associative	Maths Y7 C4
average	Maths Y9 C4, Y10 C4
circumference	Maths Y8 C4, Y10 C3
co-interior	Maths Y8 C2
coefficient	Maths Y10 C1
commutative	Maths Y7 C1
compare	Maths Y10 C4
compound	Maths Y9 C4
construct	Maths Y9 C2
convert	Maths Y7 C2
correlation	Maths Y9 C3
corresponding	Maths Y8 C2
cosine	Maths Y10 C1
cumulative	Maths Y10 C4
currency	Maths Y10 C3
decimal	Maths Y7 C3
denominator	Maths Y7 C3
density	Maths Y10 C4
diameter	Maths Y8 C4
direct proportion	Maths Y10 C3
equation	Maths Y8 C1, Y10 C2
equivalent	Maths Y7 C3
estimate	Maths Y7 C1, Y9 C4
exchange	Maths Y10 C3
expand	Maths Y7 C4, Y9 C2
expression	Maths Y7 C4, Y10 C2
exterior	Maths Y9 C3
factor	Maths Y7 C2, Y9 C2
factorisation	Maths Y8 C1
factorise	Maths Y7 C4
formulae	Maths Y10 C2
frequency	Maths Y9 C4
function	Maths Y10 C1
gradient	Maths Y9 C1
hypotenuse	Maths Y9 C2
identity	Maths Y10 C2
improper	Maths Y7 C3
index	Maths Y10 C1
index/power	Maths Y8 C1, Y9 C1
intercept	Maths Y9 C1
interior	Maths Y9 C3
interpret	Maths Y10 C4
intersection	Maths Y9 C3
inverse	Maths Y7 C4, Y9 C1
inverse proportion	Maths Y10 C3
linear	Maths Y8 C1, Y9 C1
manipulate	Maths Y10 C2
meander	Maths Y7 C2
median	Maths Y8 C4
midpoint	Maths Y9 C1
mode	Maths Y8 C4
multiple	Maths Y7 C2, Y9 C2
multiplier	Maths Y8 C3
negative	Maths Y8 C1
numerator	Maths Y7 C3
opposite	Maths Y7 C2

Word	Subject
parallel	Maths Y8 C2, Y9 C3
percentage	Maths Y7 C4
perimeter	Maths Y7 C1, Y9 C4
perpendicular	Maths Y8 C2, Y9 C2
place value	Maths Y7 C1
plantation	Maths Y8 C3
polygon	Maths Y9 C4
power	Maths Y9 C1
prime	Maths Y8 C1
prism	Maths Y8 C3
product	Maths Y7 C2
proportion	Maths Y9 C1
proportional	Maths Y8 C3
quadratic	Maths Y9 C3, Y10 C2
quartile	Maths Y10 C4
radius	Maths Y8 C4
range	Maths Y10 C4
rate	Maths Y8 C3
ration	Maths Y8 C3, Y10 C1
rearrange	Maths Y9 C2
reciprocal	Maths Y7 C3
root	Maths Y8 C1
rounding	Maths Y7 C1, Y8 C4
sector	Maths Y8 C4
sequence	Maths Y7 C4
significant	Maths Y8 C4
simplify	Maths Y7 C3, Y10 C2
simultaneous	Maths Y9 C3, Y10 C2
sine	Maths Y10 C1
solve	Maths Y8 C1
speed	Maths Y8 C3
subject	Maths Y9 C2
sum	Maths Y7 C1
surface area	Maths Y10 C3
tangent	Maths Y10 C1
term	Maths Y7 C4
transversal	Maths Y8 C2
triangle	Maths Y9 C3
trigonometric	Maths Y10 C1
truncate	Maths Y10 C3
unit	Maths Y9 C4
vertex	Maths Y8 C2
volume	Maths Y10 C3
austerity	Media Y11 C1
authenticity	Media Y10 C2
blockbuster	Media Y11 C1
broadsheet	Media Y10 C4
catharsis	Media Y10 C3
consumerism	Media Y10 C1
convergence	Media Y10 C3
demographics	Media Y9 C4
editorial	Media Y10 C4
explicit	Media Y9 C2
focus group	Media Y9 C4
franchise	Media Y10 C3, Y11 C1
horizontal	Media Y9 C3
hybridity	Media Y9 C1

Word	Subject
ideologies	Media Y9 C4
implicit	Media Y9 C2
integration	Media Y9 C3
intertextuality	Media Y9 C1
jingles	Media Y10 C2
manufactured	Media Y10 C2
mediation	Media Y9 C2
millennials	Media Y10 C3
monopoly	Media Y9 C3
narratology	Media Y9 C1
niche	Media Y10 C1
nostalgia	Media Y10 C1
oligopoly	Media Y9 C3
op-ed	Media Y10 C4
playlisting	Media Y10 C2
psychographic	Media Y9 C4
representation	Media Y9 C2
self-regulation	Media Y9 C3
social realism	Media Y11 C1
statutory regulation	Media Y9 C3
tabloid	Media Y10 C4
theoretical	Media Y9 C1
toxic masculinity	Media Y9 C2
vertical erosion	Media Y9 C3
voyeurism	Media Y10 C1
à l'hôtel	MFL Y10 C1
activités	MFL Y8 C3
ambitions	MFL Y10 C3
anniversaire	MFL Y7 C1
au restaurant	MFL Y8 C2, Y10 C1
aussi… que	MFL Y8 C4
c'était catastrophique	MFL Y10 C1
ce qui me préoccupe	MFL Y10 C4
chanter	MFL Y7 C4
cheveux	MFL Y8 C1
comme casse-croute	MFL Y11 C2
conjonctions	MFL Y8 C1
couleurs	MFL Y7 C1
d'où vient ton tee-shirt	MFL Y10 C4
derrière	MFL Y7 C2
des vacances de rêve	MFL Y10 C1
dessous	MFL Y7 C2
devant	MFL Y7 C2
devoirs	MFL Y7 C3
école primaire	MFL Y9 C3
écouter	MFL Y8 C1
en été	MFL Y7 C4
en hiver	MFL Y7 C4
en route	MFL Y10 C1
en ville	MFL Y7 C2
endroits	MFL Y9 C4
entre	MFL Y7 C2
faire	MFL Y7 C3
faire du bénévolat	MFL Y10 C4
félicitations	MFL Y10 C2
habiter	MFL Y7 C2, Y9 C4
internet	MFL Y9 C2

Word	Subject
je voudrais	MFL Y9 C4
jouer	MFL Y7 C4
journée	MFL Y7 C3
jours	MFL Y7 C1
l'uniforme scolaire	MFL Y9 C3
l'amitié	MFL Y11 C3
l'avenir	MFL Y8 C4
l'emploi du temps	MFL Y9 C3
l'orientation	MFL Y10 C3, Y11 C1
la derniére	MFL Y8 C3
la famille	MFL Y11 C3
la fréquence	MFL Y8 C2
la lecture	MFL Y9 C2
la musique	MFL Y9 C2
la nourriture	MFL Y8 C2
la région	MFL Y9 C4
la santé	MFL Y9 C3
la vie quotidienne	MFL Y10 C2
le meilleur	MFL Y9 C4, Y10 C1, C2
le projets	MFL Y9 C4
le règlement scolaire	MFL Y9 C3
le succès	MFL Y9 C3
les adjectifs de personnalité	MFL Y11 C3
les ambitions	MFL Y11 C1
les courses	MFL Y8 C2
les destinations	MFL Y8 C3
les directions	MFL Y9 C4
les émissions de télé	MFL Y9 C2
les fêtes en France	MFL Y10 C2
les gadgets	MFL Y8 C4
les grands événements	MFL Y10 C4
les langues	MFL Y8 C3
les magasins	MFL Y8 C2, Y10 C2
les pays	MFL Y8 C3
les professions	MFL Y10 C3
les repas	MFL Y8 C2
les repas de fêtes	MFL Y10 C2
les traits de personnalité	MFL Y11 C3
les transports	MFL Y8 C3
les vacances passées	MFL Y10 C1
les vêtements	MFL Y10 C2
lire	MFL Y7 C4
ma description physique	MFL Y11 C3
manger	MFL Y7 C3
matières	MFL Y7 C3
matin	MFL Y7 C3
mes rêves	MFL Y8 C4
moins ... que	MFL Y8 C4
mois	MFL Y7 C1
mon argent de poche	MFL Y8 C4
mon boulot dans le tourisme	MFL Y10 C3
mon métier de rêve	MFL Y11 C1
mon stage	MFL Y10 C3
mon téléphone portable	MFL Y9 C2
nombres	MFL Y7 C1
notre planète	MFL Y10 C4
on peut faire	MFL Y9 C4

Word	Subject
opinion	MFL Y8 C1
ou ta mère	MFL Y11 C1
parler de son enfance	MFL Y11 C3
parler de sport	MFL Y9 C2
passe-temps	MFL Y9 C2
passer	MFL Y9 C1
personnel	MFL Y8 C1
petit déjeuner	MFL Y11 C2
plus ... que	MFL Y8 C4
pour la fête	MFL Y8 C2
pourquoi	MFL Y7 C3
protéger l' environnement	MFL Y10 C4
q'est ce que tu prends comme	MFL Y11 C2
qu'est ce que tu bois	MFL Y11 C2
qu'est ce que tu mange	MFL Y11 C2
qu'est ce que tu manges le soir	MFL Y11 C2
qu'est ce que tu manges pour midi	MFL Y11 C2
quel est le métier de ton père	MFL Y11 C1
quel métier voulez-vous suivre	MFL Y11 C1
quel temps	MFL Y8 C1
rencontrer	MFL Y7 C1
repas et nourriture	MFL Y10 C2
rester	MFL Y7 C4
retrouver	MFL Y9 C1
rigoler	MFL Y9 C1
routine	MFL Y7 C3
s'entendre bien	MFL Y9 C1
s'occuper de	MFL Y9 C1
salutations	MFL Y7 C1
se disputer avec	MFL Y9 C1
sortir	MFL Y9 C1
sous	MFL Y7 C2
tous les jours	MFL Y7 C4
travailler	MFL Y8 C1
un entretien d'embauche	MFL Y10 C3
une école bien équipé	MFL Y9 C3
une invitation	MFL Y8 C2
yeux	MFL Y8 C1
accent	Music Y10 C3
accidental	Music Y9 C2
articulation	Music Y10 C3
backbeat	Music Y9 C4
bridge	Music Y9 C4
chorus	Music Y9 C4
cresendo	Music Y10 C1
delay	Music Y9 C3
diminuendo	Music Y10 C1
distortion	Music Y9 C3
dynamic	Music Y9 C2
dynamics: forte	Music Y10 C1
dynamics: mezzo forte	Music Y10 C1
dynamics: mezzo piano	Music Y10 C1
dynamics: piano	Music Y10 C1
fortissimo	Music Y10 C1
genre	Music Y9 C1
harmony	Music Y9 C1
instrumentation	Music Y9 C1

Word	Subject
introduction	Music Y9 C4
melody	Music Y9 C1
ornamentation	Music Y10 C3
projection	Music Y9 C3
reverb	Music Y9 C3
rhythm	Music Y9 C1
structure	Music Y9 C4
syncopation	Music Y9 C4
tempo	Music Y9 C1
tempo: accelerando	Music Y10 C2
tempo: adagio	Music Y10 C2
tempo: allegro	Music Y10 C2
tempo: andante	Music Y10 C2
tempo: presto	Music Y10 C2
tempo: rubato	Music Y10 C2
texture	Music Y9 C2
texture: a cappella	Music Y10 C4
texture: homophonic	Music Y10 C4
texture: monophonic	Music Y10 C4
texture: polyphonic	Music Y10 C4
timbre	Music Y9 C2
tonality: dominant	Music Y11 C1
tonality: major	Music Y11 C1
tonality: minor	Music Y11 C1
tonality: pentatonic	Music Y11 C1
tonality: tonic	Music Y11 C1
verse	Music Y9 C4
abduction	PE & Sport Y7 C2
abrasion	PE & Sport Y10 C1
acute	PE & Sport Y10 C2
adduction	PE & Sport Y7 C2
aerobic	PE & Sport Y8 C1
agonist	PE & Sport Y7 C3
anaerobic	PE & Sport Y8 C1
analytical	PE & Sport Y10 C4
antagonist	PE & Sport Y7 C3
antagonistic	PE & Sport Y7 C3
anxiety	PE & Sport Y9 C4
appendicular	PE & Sport Y9 C1
arousal	PE & Sport Y9 C4
axial	PE & Sport Y9 C1
balance	PE & Sport Y10 C4
carbohydrates	PE & Sport Y8 C4
cardiac	PE & Sport Y7 C3
cardiac output	PE & Sport Y8 C1
cardiorespiratory	PE & Sport Y9 C3
cardiovascular	PE & Sport Y7 C1
cathartic	PE & Sport Y9 C3
chronic	PE & Sport Y10 C2
circumduction	PE & Sport Y7 C2
concentric	PE & Sport Y9 C2
consultation	PE & Sport Y8 C2
continuous	PE & Sport Y8 C3
contraction	PE & Sport Y9 C2
contusion	PE & Sport Y10 C1
dynamic	PE & Sport Y10 C1
eccentric	PE & Sport Y9 C2
endurance	PE & Sport Y10 C4
enzyme	PE & Sport Y7 C4
extension	PE & Sport Y7 C2
extrinsic	PE & Sport Y9 C4
fat	PE & Sport Y8 C4
fatigue	PE & Sport Y9 C3
flexibility	PE & Sport Y7 C1
flexion	PE & Sport Y7 C2
frequency	PE & Sport Y8 C3
gastrocnemius	PE & Sport Y9 C1
glycogen	PE & Sport Y8 C4
hamstrings	PE & Sport Y9 C1
hormone	PE & Sport Y7 C4
hypertrophy	PE & Sport Y8 C1
imagery	PE & Sport Y10 C1
incentive	PE & Sport Y8 C2
intensity	PE & Sport Y8 C3
intrinsic motivation	PE & Sport Y9 C4
involuntary	PE & Sport Y7 C3
isometric	PE & Sport Y9 C2
isotonic	PE & Sport Y9 C2
latissimus dorsi	PE & Sport Y9 C1
longevity	PE & Sport Y7 C1
macronutrient	PE & Sport Y8 C4
micronutrient	PE & Sport Y8 C4
moderation	PE & Sport Y10 C3
muscular strength	PE & Sport Y7 C1
optimum	PE & Sport Y9 C4
Osgood-Schlatter's disease	PE & Sport Y10 C2
osteoporosis	PE & Sport Y10 C1
physiological	PE & Sport Y9 C4
pilates	PE & Sport Y8 C3
plateauing	PE & Sport Y9 C3
pliability	PE & Sport Y10 C1
plyometric	PE & Sport Y10 C4
posture	PE & Sport Y9 C2
power	PE & Sport Y10 C4
progression	PE & Sport Y10 C3
protein	PE & Sport Y8 C4
protocol	PE & Sport Y8 C2
psychological	PE & Sport Y7 C1
quadriceps	PE & Sport Y9 C1
regression	PE & Sport Y10 C3
reliability	PE & Sport Y8 C2
respiratory	PE & Sport Y7 C4
reversibility	PE & Sport Y10 C3
rotation	PE & Sport Y7 C2
specificity	PE & Sport Y10 C3
spinning	PE & Sport Y8 C3
sprain	PE & Sport Y10 C2
strain	PE & Sport Y10 C2
strength	PE & Sport Y10 C4
stroke volume	PE & Sport Y8 C1
tendonitis	PE & Sport Y10 C2
thermoregulation	PE & Sport Y9 C3
tidal volume	PE & Sport Y7 C4
validity	PE & Sport Y8 C2

Word	Subject
variables	PE & Sport Y8 C2
variance	PE & Sport Y10 C3
vasoconstriction	PE & Sport Y7 C4
vasodilation	PE & Sport Y7 C4
vital capacity	PE & Sport Y8 C1
VO2 max	PE & Sport Y9 C3
voluntary	PE & Sport Y7 C3
wellbeing	PE & Sport Y7 C1
yoga	PE & Sport Y8 C3
batch production	Product Design word bank
bending	Product Design word bank
biomass	Product Design word bank
building line	Product Design word bank
carbon footprint	Product Design word bank
casting	Product Design word bank
client profile	Product Design word bank
client/user	Product Design word bank
compression	Product Design word bank
conductivity	Product Design word bank
continuous production	Product Design word bank
design brief	Product Design word bank
designs	Product Design word bank
development	Product Design word bank
draft angle	Product Design word bank
ductility	Product Design word bank
ecological footprint	Product Design word bank
elasticity	Product Design word bank
employee exploitation	Product Design word bank
evaluate	Product Design word bank
fair trade	Product Design word bank
fixture	Product Design word bank
geothermal	Product Design word bank
hardness	Product Design word bank
heater element	Product Design word bank
HIPS	Product Design word bank
hydroelectric	Product Design word bank
iterations	Product Design word bank
jig	Product Design word bank
labour costs	Product Design word bank
lever	Product Design word bank
life-cycle analysis	Product Design word bank
malleability	Product Design word bank
manufacture	Product Design word bank
market pull	Product Design word bank
mass production	Product Design word bank
modelling	Product Design word bank
moulding	Product Design word bank
non-renewable energy	Product Design word bank
oil/gas/coal	Product Design word bank
one-off production	Product Design word bank
planning	Product Design word bank
platen	Product Design word bank
polymerisation	Product Design word bank
primary research	Product Design word bank
prototype	Product Design word bank
PVC	Product Design word bank
release agent	Product Design word bank

Word	Subject
renewable energy sources	Product Design word bank
research	Product Design word bank
secondary research	Product Design word bank
shear	Product Design word bank
situation	Product Design word bank
solar panels	Product Design word bank
specification	Product Design word bank
strength	Product Design word bank
sustainability	Product Design word bank
synthetic	Product Design word bank
tension	Product Design word bank
thermoforming polymers	Product Design word bank
tolerance	Product Design word bank
torsion	Product Design word bank
toughness	Product Design word bank
vacuum forming	Product Design word bank
vacuum pump	Product Design word bank
volume	Product Design word bank
wasting process	Product Design word bank
wave energy	Product Design word bank
wind turbines	Product Design word bank
abortion	RS Y9 C2
absolute poverty	RS Y10 C2
adultery	RS Y9 C3
afterlife	RS Y9 C2
agnostic	RS Y8 C3
aid	RS Y7 C3
akhirah/afterlife	RS Y11 C1
al-qada/predestination	RS Y11 C1
Allah	RS Y8 C2, Y11 C1
angels	RS Y11 C1
anti-Semitism	RS Y8 C2
atheism	RS Y7 C1
atheist	RS Y8 C3
atonement	RS Y9 C1
baptism	RS Y9 C4, Y10 C4
belief	RS Y7 C1
Bible	RS Y7 C2
caste system	RS Y7 C4
censorship	RS Y10 C2
cohabitation	RS Y9 C3
commitment	RS Y9 C3
conscience	RS Y7 C1
contraception	RS Y9 C3
conviction	RS Y10 C2
creation	RS Y7 C2
determinism	RS Y10 C3
dharma	RS Y7 C4
discrimination	RS Y8 C2
divorce	RS Y9 C3
ecumenism	RS Y9 C4, Y10 C4
environmental	RS Y9 C2
equality	RS Y8 C4, Y9 C3
eucharist	RS Y9 C4, Y10 C4
euthanasia	RS Y9 C2
evangelism	RS Y9 C1, C4, Y10 C4
evil	RS Y10 C3

Word	Subject
evolution	RS Y8 C3, Y9 C2
extremism	RS Y10 C2
forgiveness	RS Y10 C3
genocide	RS Y8 C2
ghetto	RS Y8 C2
gurdwara	RS Y8 C4
guru	RS Y8 C4
halal	RS Y10 C1
harem	RS Y10 C1
Holocaust	RS Y8 C2
immanence	RS Y11 C1
incarnation	RS Y7 C2, Y9 C1
jihad	RS Y10 C1
justice (social)	RS Y10 C2, C3
karma	RS Y7 C4
knowledge	RS Y7 C1
langar	RS Y8 c7
moksha	RS Y7 C4
morality	RS Y7 C1, Y10 C3
mosque	RS Y8 C1, Y10 C1
omnibenevolent	RS Y8 C3
omnipotence	RS Y9 C1, Y8 C3
omnipresent	RS Y8 C1
omniscience	RS Y8 C3
omniscient	RS Y8 C1
parable	RS Y7 C2
persecution	RS Y8 C2, Y9 C4, Y10 C4
philosophy	RS Y7 C1
pilgrimage	RS Y7 C4, Y9 C4, Y10 C4
poverty	RS Y7 C3
prejudice	RS Y8 C2, Y10 C2
prophethood	RS Y10 C1, Y11 C1
punishment	RS Y10 C3
reincarnation	RS Y7 C4
responsibilities	RS Y7 C3, Y9 C3
resurrection	RS Y9 C1
rites of passage	RS Y7 C4
roles	RS Y9 C3
sacrament	RS Y9 C1, Y9 C4, Y10 C4
salvation	RS Y7 C2
samsara	RS Y7 C4
sermon	RS Y7 C2
sewa	RS Y8 C4
sharia	RS Y10 C1
Shi'a	RS Y8 C1
Sikhism	RS Y8 c8
sin	RS Y10 C3

Word	Subject
soul	RS Y9 C2
suffering	RS Y10 C3
Sunni	RS Y8 C1
sustainability	RS Y9 C2
tawhid	RS Y8 C1, Y10 C1, Y11 C1
testament	RS Y7 C2
theism	RS Y7 C1
theist	RS Y8 C3
transcendence	RS Y11 C1
trinity	RS Y9 C1
wealth	RS Y7 C3
wisdom	RS Y7 C1
arrangement	Science word bank
balanced	Science word bank
cause	Science word bank
characteristics	Science word bank
classify	Science word bank
collision	Science word bank
common	Science word bank
conservation	Science word bank
constant	Science word bank
direction	Science word bank
discovery	Science word bank
effect	Science word bank
equation	Science word bank
equivalent	Science word bank
factor	Science word bank
flows	Science word bank
function	Science word bank
linear	Science word bank
magnitude	Science word bank
measure	Science word bank
practical	Science word bank
property	Science word bank
proportional	Science word bank
qualitative	Science word bank
quantitative	Science word bank
random	Science word bank
rate	Science word bank
ratio	Science word bank
reaction	Science word bank
regular	Science word bank
relationship	Science word bank
stored	Science word bank
structure	Science word bank
theory	Science word bank
transfer	Science word bank

Chapter 15. Staff development

Let's return once again to the tree analogy. In order to firmly embed a whole-school approach to disciplinary literacy, we must consider the underlying roots necessary to ensure that literacy can flourish. A strong culture of staff development is needed to sustain any school improvement strategy. Every teacher and leader must have an unwavering commitment to continuous improvement, and I believe this can most effectively be supported through the coaching model explained in this chapter.

Alongside an effective model for pedagogical improvement, there must be opportunities for all teachers to develop their curricular knowledge and consider how best to deliver the curriculum in the context of their own classroom. Teacher improvement strategies often become focused on the pedagogical methods adopted in classrooms, without considering the quality of the curriculum content that teachers are expected to deliver, which could be beyond their control. A differentiated curriculum path sets up students with weaker literacy skills to achieve mediocrity at best. The recent focus on Rosenshine's principles of instruction has been incredibly beneficial, but we must not neglect Engelmann's original focus on the marriage between curriculum and pedagogy.

It is also essential for teachers to have a clear understanding of which children are furthest behind in their classes; they must prepare lessons that target those key students in ways that give them the best possible chance of success. Rather than wasting preparation time by creating differentiated resources for these students, teachers must plan how they can be drawn into the most crucial points of a lesson. This will be further explored later in this chapter.

Developing all staff through practical CPD and one-to-one coaching

Steve Margetts, before taking over as principal of Torquay Academy, carried out an extraordinary amount of research into education and leadership, part of which involved spending time with Doug Lemov in the US. Since 2005, Lemov has been documenting the actions of teachers who achieve excellence with their classes in challenging environments. Through his observations of thousands of lessons, he was able to pinpoint what these teachers did to facilitate success; he came up with useful terminology to label and characterise what had always been considered an indefinable art, or had been unhelpfully described in broad and lengthy Ofsted criteria. *Teach Like a Champion*[67] is one of the most illuminating books I've read about education: it helped me to understand why what I did in my classroom when nobody was watching worked well, and why the 'showcase' lessons I designed for observations were unnecessary.

Steve was also heavily influenced by Paul Bambrick-Santoyo and his book *Leverage Leadership*.[68] Anyone involved in developing school staff should read this book. Before we embarked on the coaching programme at Torquay Academy, every coach was given the second chapter of the book to read. It convincingly illustrates the power of incremental coaching: immediate feedback that recognises specific points of success, identifies one precise area of improvement and provides opportunities for practice before the teacher heads back into the classroom. Bambrick-Santoyo claims this method will 'drive as much improvement in a year as most schools do in 20'. I worked in a 'requires improvement' school that introduced incremental coaching and I can attest to its power in creating change, especially compared with my previous experience of CPD.

Teach Like a Champion provided the common language needed to ensure that all teachers were aware of the specific strategies that would have the most impact. This was especially helpful in our context at Torquay Academy, where almost half of children are classed as 'disadvantaged'. We launched our coaching programme at our first ever

67. Lemov, D. (2010) *Teach Like a Champion*, Jossey-Bass
68. Bambrick-Santoyo, P with Peiser, B. (2012) *Leverage Leadership: a practical guide to building exceptional schools*, Jossey-Bass

'teaching and learning conference', held at a local hotel on the first day back in September 2015. This event had a huge impact. It established a culture of shared values around teaching and, most importantly, set the expectation that everyone can and should make improving their classroom practice their top priority. Staff rotated around workshops focused on 'threshold', 'do now' (the first activity students complete when they arrive in class), 'turn and talk' and 'cold call'. We watched videos of excellent practice, then worked in groups to script and try out different classroom scenarios. This felt a little alien at first, but it was blindingly obvious that this is how CPD for teachers should look and feel. The conversations that resulted from the practice elements were the most valuable because experienced teachers were able to share their expertise with NQTs. Relationships were built on a shared appreciation of what effective teaching should look like. Most importantly, those children who find school challenging now have teachers trained in the methods that support their learning most effectively.

The coaching that followed this conference was grounded in this shared understanding. As a coach, my initial focus was on the starts of lessons and those two key areas that we had established as a school priority. First, the idea that teachers should greet their students warmly at the door as they arrive, with an eye on the classroom and on the corridor. Second, that all students should have a silent activity to begin as soon as they arrive. Today, this involves low-stakes retrieval practice based on knowledge organisers, but from the introduction of the activity the point was that 'every second counts' and students should be settled and occupied from the moment they arrive in class.

To many experienced teachers, there is nothing revolutionary about starting lessons in this way. However, as I soon discovered, every teacher has different experiences of teacher training, different expectations of their students and different perceptions of how lessons should begin. Coaching provided a non-threatening means of honing this micro-element of teaching. For some, it was simply a case of organisation: getting to the point where all the resources were readily available so the teacher could stand at the door to greet students. For others, it was a case of establishing behaviour expectations and adjusting students' expectations around the start of lessons. This was what I found most challenging with my own classes: I joined Torquay Academy when behaviour expectations were not yet well established after years of 'special measures' and underachievement. It was hard work, but the consistency with which these practices have been implemented across the school has made it so much easier to remind students that *this* is how we do things around here. Steve has written about our journey in coming out of special measures in his book *Everyone Succeeds*,[69] which covers in greater detail how the coaching process was established, as well as other school improvement strategies.

Key to the development of our coaching process was Steve's relationship with Andy Buck, a well-established school leader and the founder of Leadership Matters (Andy was also a director of the National College for School Leadership). Alongside Nichole Sanders, Torquay Academy's assistant principal for teaching and learning, they developed a simplified version of Bambrick-Santoyo's model to form the basis for coaching conversations. This ASAP model has provided consistency across our school, allowing for recognition of what is going well, the setting of agreed targets for improvement and the practice of agreed strategies in a safe environment.

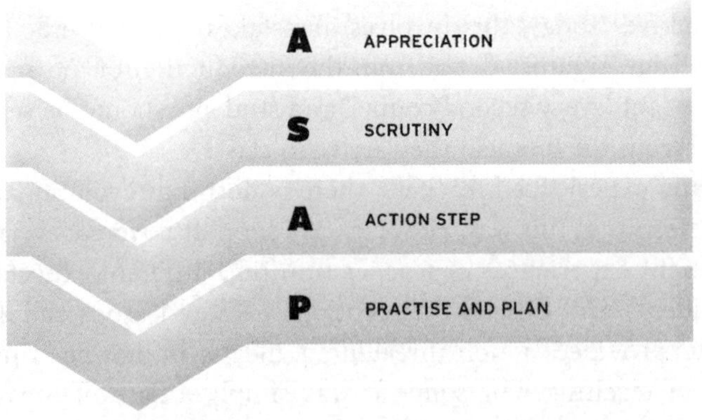

69. Margetts, S. (2018) *Everyone Succeeds*, John Catt

The straightforward sequence of steps in the ASAP model ensures that, rather than the template of praise and criticism that is often the outcome of traditional performance management observations, a more collaborative and organic discussion can take place. The coachee can play a role in identifying which element of their teaching they would like to work on.

Setting up the coaching system, particularly with the commitment to weekly coaching sessions, required a significant financial investment. Lead practitioners were employed to carry out coaching alongside every member of the senior leadership team. This investment signalled to staff that their development was a key priority and the coaching model would be their primary source of professional development. Significant savings were made by cutting back on all but the most crucial external training; expensive courses from which learnings were often poorly applied in practice were no longer an option. The investment was instead made in what happens day-to-day in the classroom.

A blueprint for how a coaching conversation might unfold is presented on page 36. This blueprint identifies the key areas of focus, which have now evolved to specifically reference the minutiae of the modelling process. This is key to developing disciplinary literacy, as staff are given the opportunity to work on specific elements of the modelling process within their coaching sessions. Key questions and points of practice are identified in the blueprint, so coach and coachee both have a crystal clear idea of what effective modelling should look like. Even the most expert teachers are able to find areas where they can develop and improve.

Once the coaching system had been launched, we were visited by Peter Matthews, who carried out an evaluation of our incremental coaching during 2016. A detailed report on his findings was published by Ambition School Leadership (now the Ambition Institute) in 2016. Matthews concluded: 'The fundamental link that has been established between training, incremental coaching and improving the quality and consistency of instruction should not be ignored.'[70] It is well worth referring to the report in order to find out more about teacher perceptions of coaching and the evidence of its impact. It has now been five years since the original ASAP model was developed and Andy Buck recently published a book on his BASIC coaching framework, a more evolved version of the original model.[71]

Building subject expertise among staff and planning for small successes with key students

It is absolutely vital that curriculum teams meet on a regular basis, in order to share their passion for their subject and discuss the most effective methods of engaging key students in their classes. Too often, departmental meetings happen sporadically and end up being a discussion of administration issues. Notices and admin should be delivered through weekly bulletins, but meeting time should, as far as possible, be dedicated to discussing the upcoming curriculum and allowing teachers to consider the best ways to implement this in their lessons. This will look different in different subjects, but most usefully it will consider the questions to be asked of students to embed understanding of a key concept.

At Torquay Academy, Harrison Littler and Jamie Engineer have developed curriculum planners to facilitate discussion within department meetings. These include week-by-week curriculum plans, as well as space for seating plans and key information about each class. Teachers then discuss the upcoming curriculum for each year group and take time to record key actions for the classes they have chosen to focus on that week. Opposite is an example of how this might look.

70. Matthews, P. (2016) *Incremental Coaching in Schools: small steps to professional mastery – an evaluation and guide for leaders*, Ambition School Leadership. Retrieved from: https://s3.eu-west-2.amazonaws.com/ambition-institute/documents/Incremental_coaching_-_full_report.pdf (accessed 04.11.20)

71. Buck, A. (2020) *The BASIC Coaching Method*, Cadogan Press

Teacher reflection and action planning	
Subject CPD (notes from curriculum briefing. Planning and scripting for the week ahead)	
Both Kelsey and Jacob suffer from low self-esteem and often attempt to 'opt out' of answers. Structuring the lessons like this will allow them to achieve success, which can be followed up with a positive phone call home.	
Student progress reflection (individuals/groups/Narrowing the Gap students)	**Curriculum reflection** (quality and appropriateness of lesson resources and activities)
Actions for upcoming lessons (opportunities to e.g. adapt lessons, target questions) *In Monday's lesson, I will ask Kelsey to tell me how Macbeth 'disrupted the natural order' within the play. I will expect her to use the phrase 'committed regicide' and will ask her to extend her response by relating this to the 'great chain of being'. Both of these concepts will be part of the 'do now', so I will refer her back to this part of her exercise book if she is unsure.* *In Tuesday's lesson, when we are making our essay plans, I will ask Jacob to remind me of the explanations Kelsey gave yesterday so that he includes them in his plan. I will choose his work to show call and celebrate where he has used these terms, then give him pointers as to how he can make his writing even better.*	**Actions for subject CPD** (suggested changes to lesson resources and curriculum maps) Note: this is written in full sentences for clarity, but it is anticipated that teachers will make brief notes on a range of children

This is particularly important for those students with weaker literacy skills. If they are behind in a subject, their teacher needs the time and space to think carefully about how to draw them into pivotal moments in the lesson, in a way that ensures they are most likely to succeed. Daniel Willingham refers to the importance of children experiencing small successes in their thinking that motivate them to make further progress in a subject.[72] If all their teachers planned for these small moments of

72. Willingham, DT. (2009) *Why Don't Students Like School?*, Jossey-Bass

success, their experience of school would likely be very different. Of course, this will be easier for some teachers than others: an RS teacher will see many more students in a week than a maths teacher. However, we all know those students who are furthest behind and are the most difficult to engage. We might not be able to target them all every week, but if we are teaching the same lesson to several classes then the questioning can remain the same for those key characters.

Departmental meetings are vital to develop challenging, knowledge-rich curricula that grow and change organically as teachers develop and become more aspirational in terms of what can be achieved. Meetings are also essential when resources are centrally planned, so that any gaps in staff subject knowledge and potential misconceptions can be addressed.

Chapter 16. Building a reading and writing culture

The development of staff paves the way for positive change to a school's literacy culture. In schools where each subject discipline is valued for the unique opportunities and challenges it offers in relation to literacy, staff are far more likely to be receptive to creating an environment that allows those students who struggle most with literacy to thrive. In this chapter, we will explore how school leaders can foster a culture underpinned by reading and writing.

Developing a reading culture

Although disciplinary literacy focuses on reading in each of the subject disciplines, it is not always practical or beneficial for students to read in every lesson. Rich access to reading material needs to be part of a balanced and well-rounded curriculum, and supplemented by reading that a child chooses to do because it is enjoyable. In chapter 2, I discussed the benefits to children of reading a wide range of stories that reflect their own lives and the lives of people they are less familiar with. This helps them to build a sense of their own identity and introduces them to alternative experiences, weaving a rich tapestry of histories, cultures and places, real and imagined. Fundamentally, we want children to read because it will unlock their educational potential. But, over and above this, reading can unlock their potential as people. The agony and the ecstasy of the teenage experience can be navigated more smoothly when you are not alone and books can, at times, provide the company that is most needed: someone who has been there before and can hold your hand as you discover who you want to become.

We have all read the statistics about the number of children who grow up in houses without books, making a dedicated library space in school even more important. A space like this is vital to fostering a school reading culture and it must be stocked with books that can be accessed by children of all reading abilities. The publishing company Barrington Stoke[73] specialises in books that can be accessed by children with lower reading levels, particularly those with dyslexia, but are not packaged to look different. The ideal library should contain a mix of popular titles designed to draw in reluctant but able readers, more challenging 'next steps' novels for children who already have a passion for reading, and titles that can be accessed and enjoyed by those who find reading difficult. This requires a significant investment of time and expertise, and it is important that a school librarian with a deep knowledge of young adult fiction is available to provide guidance and support to students and staff.

Great School Libraries

One in eight primary and secondary schools do not have access to a designated library area on-site, according to the Great School Libraries campaign.[74] Schools where a quarter or more of the pupils are eligible for free school meals are 11 percentage points less likely to have access to a designated library area on-site than those schools where fewer than one in 10 pupils are eligible.

The 'library lesson'

All students should have regular, dedicated time to visit the library. Most schools appreciate this and dutifully timetable a 'library lesson'. Sometimes these sessions work brilliantly; at other times they lack structure and are an opportunity for students to mess around or merely pretend to read as they have mouthed conversations with friends. Teachers can find these

73. www.barringtonstoke.co.uk

74. Great School Libraries/BMG Research. (2019) *Research Report: national survey to scope school library provision in England, Northern Ireland, and Wales.* Retrieved from: https://d824397c-0ce2-4fc6-b5c4-8d2e4de5b242.filesusr.com/ugd/8d6dfb_8b81a7c94c2c4c4a970265496f42307a.pdf (accessed 19.09.20)

lessons very stressful. If they get fed up with trying in vain to encourage/coerce children into reading, they might give up and use the time to get on with some marking or work on their laptop.

If a reading culture is not yet well established, it is unrealistic to expect children to immediately sit down and begin reading their books in silence. Children will either accept whatever punishment comes from not having a book, or carry the same tattered book around and bring it out in every library lesson as a prop to support their facade of engagement. To add structure to lessons, it is important first of all to establish a reading curriculum. Traditionally, library lessons do not have a specific curriculum, as the intention is for children to read their own books and effectively create their 'own' curriculum. Unfortunately, many children lack the motivation, engagement and skills to devise this curriculum for themselves; the shelves full of books might not spark awe and wonder but rather fear, dread or, worst of all, absolutely nothing.

A reading curriculum for the library lesson must be devised alongside the English curriculum, and used as an opportunity to enrich and widen students' appreciation of the texts studied in the classroom. For example, as I mentioned in chapter 2, the first book read by our Year 7s is *Lord of the Flies*. As a dystopian novel, it is the perfect springboard for reading a whole range of dystopian novels aimed at young people and adults.

The reading curriculum must be designed to allow all children to independently read books that are at their level, and to have a clear understanding of the books they can move on to when they are ready for the next level. I am a strong advocate for teaching to the top and removing the ceiling for lower-ability children, but independent reading is one area where giving a book that is too challenging will benefit no one. In a classroom environment where reading is guided by the teacher, the sky is the limit, but when it comes to independent reading we want children to enjoy the experience – so much so that they take the book home because they want to find out what happens next. This is no small ask in this age of distraction, so the book needs to be accessible and engaging.

To that end, with the support of our school librarian, I have devised 'reading mountains', which organise books into the theme or genre of the text studied within English. The most accessible books are at ground level. They become increasingly challenging until students reach the top of the mountain, where they will find those classic novels written at an adult level:

It is important, however, that all children gain a sense of the entire mountain. Therefore, a short extract from each book has been organised into a library workbook for use at the start of the lesson. On arrival, students are expected to read that lesson's extract. They are then asked to write a short description inspired by an accompanying image; a vocabulary bank is provided to support their writing. The vocabulary bank and images all feed into the wider narrative of the dystopian genre and ultimately feed back into students' appreciation of *Lord of the Flies*. Situating the text in this broader context also helps students to make links between the films or television programmes they may have watched and build up their schema of knowledge surrounding this topic.

The ability to make connections such as these is fundamental to all learning and, as I have discussed elsewhere in this book, there is much more that can be done to capitalise on the links between the subject disciplines. In the case of dystopian fiction, the more children read, the more likely they are to tune in to the representation of religion, for example. In some dystopian texts, religion is presented as an oppressive force that is part of what Louis Althusser described as a 'state apparatus of ideology'.[75] In other texts, religion is a pathway to redemption. Reading opens the door to this broad background knowledge, but the door will remain firmly closed for children who don't read.

Reading at home

The ultimate remedy for any child who is behind with their reading progress is to spend time reading outside school. If there is one thing a school can do to narrow the attainment gap, it would be to facilitate this for all children who are struggling academically. It is, however, a challenging goal to achieve. So challenging that many schools might set the broad expectation that children read outside school, but not collect evidence to determine that it is actually happening. There are a number of ways in which evidence could theoretically be collected – for example, asking children to write reviews when they finish books, note down key vocabulary, keep a log of the page numbers, complete quizzes, etc. All these methods have their benefits and their drawbacks. Those schools that wish to create a reading culture that involves children reading regularly at home must ultimately employ rigorous checking procedures.

If a child is asked to write a review when they have finished reading a book, there must be space within their timetable for this review to be acknowledged by the teacher. Those children who are not producing reviews, or are making a cursory effort to produce evidence of something that has not taken place, need to be identified so that conversations can take place about their reading. This is not straightforward and there can be many reasons why a child is not engaging with reading. They are far more likely to engage, however, if they know their progress will be noticed and

75. Althusser, L. (1971) 'Ideology and ideological state apparatuses', *Lenin and Philosophy and other Essays*

cared about by an adult in school. They are also more likely to engage if their parents have received support and guidance in how best to encourage their reading. At Torquay Academy, we have devised reading journals designed to encourage regular reading through the achievement of goals:

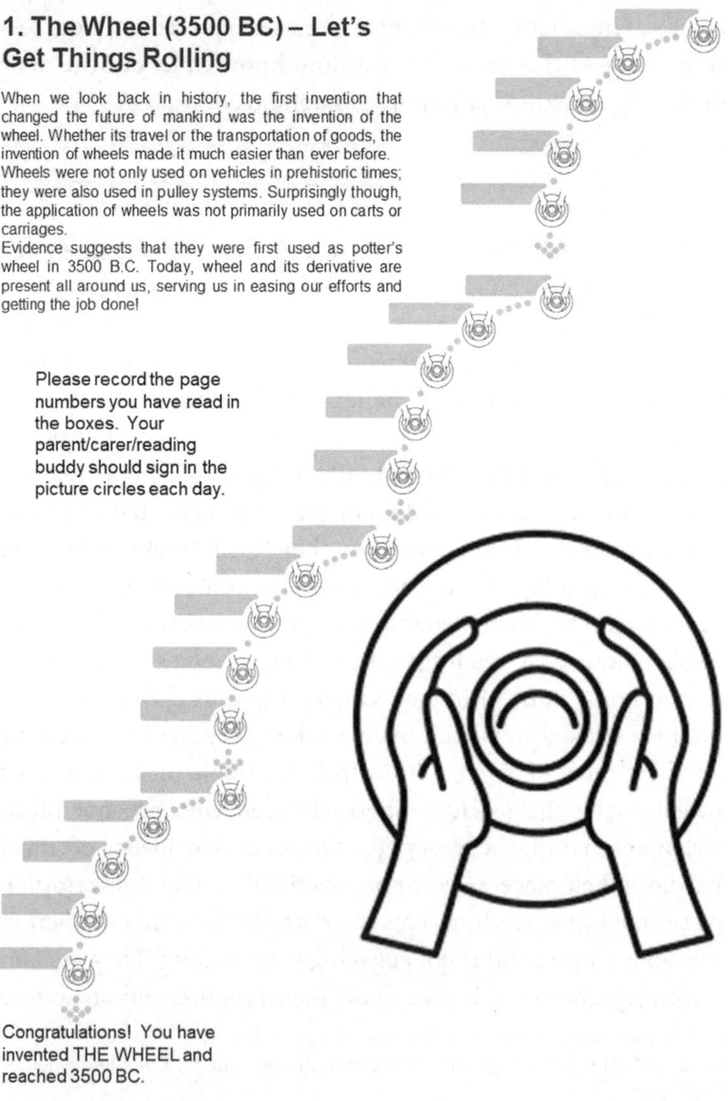

Every four weeks a child 'discovers' a new historical invention, making the connection between reading and the discovery of new and useful knowledge that has helped to create the world as we know it. Parents/carers are asked to sign the reading journal each week to confirm that their child has been reading regularly, and the child must record the pages they have read. When they reach the end of eight weeks, they show the journal to their teacher in order to be rewarded with a reading badge (from bronze through to gold). Those children who are most behind with their reading progress have two reading journals, as they have regular time in school to read one-to-one with an adult. These adults are their 'reading buddies' and they sign the journals that are kept in school. This guarantees success for children and ensures that those who receive inconsistent support at home are not prevented from participating.

Finding 'the one'

Whenever I talk to parents or children about reading, I talk about finding that 'one book' that will unlock the joy of reading for those who are reluctant. Many children grow up loving books and can't imagine why anyone would dislike reading. For these children, it is so important that their love of reading is harnessed; they must be given plenty of opportunities to move forward in their reading journey and plenty of access to new and exciting titles that will keep their passion alive. For many other children, however, reading has never been something they have engaged with or felt is 'for them'. There is nothing more rewarding for a librarian or library teacher than to recommend a book to a child like this and find that they love it and have an appetite for more. This is where an expert in young adult fiction is vital – someone who can say, 'You enjoyed *Artemis Fowl*, so how about you take a look at the Cherub series?'

We have already discussed the importance of accessibility. This is a fine balance and essentially we need to find the 'Goldilocks' of books: one that is challenging enough to support children in making progress, but not so challenging that they continually stumble over vocabulary and sentence structures that reinforce their sense of reading failure. If a child is to read independently, it stands to reason that the reading must be pleasurable, especially when books have to compete with mobile phones, tablets and consoles. It can be beneficial to have a section of the library where books are organised via accessibility and reading level. This may sound off-putting, as children will know that the section they choose from advertises their ability. Therefore, it is essential to normalise this categorisation from Year 7.

In primary school, children become very used to working through reading levels – their reading ability in comparison to their peers is no secret to them. The shame comes from an adult's reluctance to acknowledge this, perhaps by giving children little indication as to which books are likely to be accessible for them or not. Colour-coded and alphabetical organisation might feel like a logical compromise, but for children who are very weak readers it can be dismaying to have to search through hundreds of books to try to find one suitable for them; the very act of deciphering the colour code and then scanning the spines can also be cognitively demanding. The school libraries that work particularly well have a section where books are organised from least to most challenging, with the most engaging titles placed in this section. These popular books are also available in an alphabetised section, alongside some of the more adult titles that appeal to able readers. If students can't find the book they want, they are able to look it up via a system that indicates its location.

Helping children to find the book that will switch them on to reading is a complex task. In many schools, it is aspired to but never quite achieved, as all the necessary elements have not been pieced together in a way that acknowledges the challenges of creating a reading culture for all. The schools that are most successful are those that make this a key priority for school improvement and invest heavily in ensuring that the right people are given the time and resources to make it work.

Reading initiatives

Here we will consider those reading initiatives that have gained popularity and traction in recent years and discuss the conditions needed to make each scheme successful.

Drop everything and read (DEAR)

Many schools, rather than opting for dedicated library time, allocate time either between lessons or within lessons for children to drop what they are doing and read (in some cases, this occurs in addition to library time). Sometimes children read their own book that they are expected to carry with them; at other times teachers have a tub of books for children to choose from. The premise behind this is admirable: every teacher is seen to support reading and ideally will themselves read as well as the children. When DEAR works well it certainly feeds into a whole-school culture of reading. However, there are many ways in which it can fall short of aspirations. In a report, the Education Endowment Foundation questions whether every child benefits from silent reading time.[76] Do some merely go through the motions? This issue is similar to that encountered in less-than-successful library lessons.

If we fail to tackle the root causes of why a child does not choose to read and take steps to remedy this, then simply timetabling reading time will not help the children most in need of support. More than this, it will serve to widen achievement gaps and create a double disadvantage: weaker students who do not engage with DEAR cannot afford to spend valuable lesson time sitting and staring into space; meanwhile, their peers who can better afford to lose lesson time will actually enjoy the reading and benefit from it. It is unfortunate that so many initiatives put in place to support disadvantaged students actually provide greater support to their more advantaged peers and serve to widen achievement gaps.

---

76. Quigley, A and Coleman, R. (2019) *Improving Literacy in Secondary Schools: guidance report*, Education Endowment Foundation. Retrieved from: https://educationendowmentfoundation.org.uk/public/files/Publications/Literacy/EEF_KS3_KS4_LITERACY_GUIDANCE.pdf (accessed 19.09.20)

DEAR can only work if it is part of a school culture that supports children who are not engaging with reading to do so. One way to achieve this would be to ensure that reluctant readers spend DEAR time reading one-to-one with an adult; again, the culture of the school must be one in which this is normalised and children do not feel singled out or shamed for receiving this support. DEAR can send a really powerful message to the whole school community, but it has to sit on a strong foundation. It will not create a reading culture in and of itself.

Accelerated Reader

As with DEAR, in and of itself Accelerated Reader[77] will not create a reading culture. However, in my experience, the data that this software provides is invaluable: it allows those students who read regularly to be celebrated and recognised, and those students who are reluctant readers (at all ability levels) to be identified, supported and encouraged. The quizzes that students complete when they have finished reading a book are motivational and provide those small successes that Daniel Willingham has found are so valuable in engaging young people in learning.[78]

The data provided by AR essentially comes in five forms:

1. **Reading ages via an online Star Reading comprehension test**. AR facilitates the assessment of a cohort's reading age and progress as frequently as necessary, at no additional cost, through the Star Reading test. A baseline can be set when students arrive in September and follow-up testing can take place to determine their reading progress. This can be used to monitor the impact of an intervention and more generally can flag up those children who are in need of greater support.
2. **Zone of proximal development (ZPD) reading ranges**. Each child has a reading range determined by the results of their Star Reading test. This tells them the book range that is most appropriate for

77. www.renlearn.co.uk/reading
78. Willingham, DT. (2009) *Why Don't Students Like School?*, Jossey-Bass

them if they are going to make progress. I must stress that this is not a perfect system and parents and children will be put out if it is introduced as a straitjacket, as I understand has happened in some schools. What is paramount is a child's enjoyment of reading, particularly in a secondary context; it would be absolute nonsense to say they can't read the next Harry Potter book because it is not within their range. Indeed, AR recommends an approximate 60/40 split between the books read within and outside a student's ZPD range. First and foremost, the reading range is a guide and it is most relevant to struggling readers who really need to know that a book is going to be accessible for them. It is also useful for those children who are stuck in a bit of a reading rut, perhaps repeatedly choosing books that are just a bit too easy for them, because it can encourage them to branch out.

3. **Quiz scores for individual books read**. Each quiz involves between three and 20 multiple-choice questions, depending on the length of the book, and provides a score out of 10. The questions will quickly determine whether the book has been read: they are not particularly challenging but they will weed out those students who have only read the beginning or perhaps just watched the film. It is important that students take the quiz soon after they have finished reading, so regular quizzing opportunities are paramount. Feedback on the quiz is immediate and creates a buzz of satisfaction that can be capitalised upon through longer-term tracking of quiz success. The data can be fed into whole-school competitions and is a great leveller – a passed quiz is rewarding regardless of how challenging the book was, allowing weaker readers to contribute to group success on equal terms with stronger readers. This is really important in creating a culture of success around reading.
4. **Progress towards reading targets**. A child's progress toward their reading target is a useful way of determining how much time they are spending reading, in order to provide a summative view of reading success across a term. The AR system will triangulate their

reading ability and the amount of time they should spend reading per day, coming up with a number of points to be achieved (it is recommended that each student's target is checked by their teacher and adjusted if necessary). Each book is allocated a certain number of points depending on its length and challenge. Every time a child completes a book quiz, they earn points towards their target depending on the number of correct answers. It can be difficult for class teachers to scan the number of quizzes and see exactly who is reading regularly each day, but the points target, and a child's progress towards this, gives a strong indication of how much reading they are doing.

5. **Number of words read**. Just like our excellent artists, footballers and performers, we need to celebrate those who are really dazzling in terms of their reading. The term 'word millionaire' has a real kudos attached to it; in schools where this system is in place, I have seen children take their 'word millionaire' awards very seriously. AR is able to keep a running total of all the words read by children, based on their quiz results and the data held on each book.

An important element of the AR process is the way in which library stock is evaluated to determine any 'gaps' in the level of challenge. For example, if a number of children have a reading age of around nine but there are very few books that can be accessed at this level, this will be flagged up. Equally, if there are a number of able readers but few books to provide them with sufficient challenge, this will be identified. This data gives the librarian the opportunity to ensure that when restocking takes place, books can be purchased to plug the gaps.

If implemented carefully and with the correct time, personnel and resources, AR can be incredibly powerful. However, if it is allocated to an already busy teacher as an add-on to their role with little support, there is a danger that, as with DEAR, it will have a negative effect on achievement gaps. If reluctant readers are not appropriately supported, they can be left feeling that reading is just not meant for them. And if the focus is purely on celebrating 'successful' readers, then a system of meritocracy will follow: those who are already good at reading will be encouraged further, while those who struggle will remain on the outside of the process. It is very possible to have a system that appears on the surface to be working extremely well, but does little to support those who need it most and ultimately alienates them further.

Lexia PowerUp Literacy

Some children need specific reading intervention that goes right back to word- and sentence-level decoding. Our SENDCo at Torquay Academy, Eloise Jukes, has developed our use of the web-based programme Lexia PowerUp Literacy[79] to support those who are furthest behind with their reading. It quickly assesses the needs of each child and targets them with activities appropriate to their ability, effectively adopting a mastery approach as they progress through the challenges and levels. Students find the programme engaging and, as an intervention tool, it can easily be integrated into the final 20 minutes of a lesson when a group of students need literacy support but at different levels. It can also be managed by a teaching assistant, provided they have been trained in the administration and are working with small groups.

Read Write Inc. Fresh Start[80]

This is a phonics-based programme that can return students to the very beginning of the phonics journey, if that is what they need. It can be administered for groups of up to eight by a teacher or teaching assistant with the appropriate expertise. The programme is designed for the small number of pupils who are most behind with their reading, and for whom Lexia PowerUp Literacy alone is not enough to support them to make rapid progress.

79. www.lexiauk.co.uk/products/powerup
80. www.ruthmiskin.com/en/programmes/fresh-start

Lexonik

Lexonik[81] is a very effective programme that supports students' ability to break unfamiliar words into their component parts and use their understanding of etymology to extract meaning. It is a short programme of six hour-long sessions for groups of up to four. We have found that it is particularly effective when operated alongside a whole-school focus on vocabulary and explicit teaching of the components of words. It is particularly useful for older students who are still behind with their reading despite intervention in Years 7 and 8. The brevity of the programme means that, when extractions are spread over different subject areas, the impact on a student's access to the curriculum is limited.

Bedrock and Tassomai

I have grouped these two together as they are both web-based programmes designed to be accessed from home. Bedrock[82] focuses explicitly on vocabulary acquisition, while Tassomai[83] quizzes students on their knowledge of a range of subjects and can be customised with key knowledge designed by schools. Our librarian, Charlotte Aitken, has designed quizzes that combine knowledge of etymology with the vocabulary from our TA Dictionary. This supports students' literacy as well as their retrieval of key concepts across the curriculum. As discussed in chapter 5, Tassomai can be an effective replacement for knowledge organisers in science.

Tutor reading

As an example of powerful use of tutor reading, I can do no better than provide a case study of what I saw at Henley Bank High School in Gloucester, part of the Greenshaw Learning Trust, which really has tutor reading nailed.

81. www.lexonik.co.uk
82. www.bedrocklearning.org
83. www.tassomai.com

Case study: Henley Bank tutor reading programme

There is a special energy about schools that are making huge strides to improve the life chances of the young people in their communities. The senior leaders have a spring in their step, the teachers demonstrably buy into the overarching aims of those leaders, and the children clearly take pride in belonging to a place that is achieving great things. *Their* place.

Henley Bank High School is one of those schools. My headteacher asked me to respond to the school's generous open invitation to be shown its tutor reading programme, which he had seen at a By Leaders, For Leaders conference. We run a similar scheme at Torquay Academy, but we were keen to tighten up our practice. After looking through the slides put together by Greenshaw Learning Trust's Josie Mingay for the conference, it was clear that I needed to see the programme in action, particularly when I looked up the school's context and saw that it has a similar proportion of pupil premium pupils to Torquay Academy and is achieving excellent outcomes.

When I arrived at Henley Bank, I was part of a large crowd of visitors who were all keen to find out more. Josie made us very welcome as she communicated her passion for the tutor reading programme, which runs across all the schools in the trust. The idea of 7000 students all reading at the same time every day is incredibly powerful and a real achievement. Josie told us that the way in which the school day is organised is very important: five minutes have been taken from each lesson to allow for a full 25 minutes of reading at the start of the day, as well as 20 minutes for DEAR at the end of the day. It wasn't long before we were joined by headteacher Bradley Nash, who talked to us about his support for the programme and its centrality to the school's culture and ethos. Children at Henley Bank see themselves as readers and nothing is more important than those minutes of reading at the start of the day. There are no interventions, no conversations, no interruptions - just solid reading.

We were taken to see the school's 'roll call' at 8.30am, which is similar to our 'line-up'. Henley Bank is growing (the hallmark of an improving school), with around 70 pupils in Year 11 and 150 in Year 7, so the current use of the sports hall as the meeting point is not likely to last for much longer! However, for now it works extremely well as a location where tutors can check equipment and messages can be delivered. Students start the day calmly and consistently and with a positive message from their headteacher, who clearly cares about them.

Next, tutors lead students silently to their form rooms; we visitors were allowed to move freely from one class to the next. All form rooms had the following slide displayed (the books are rotated so the slide varied from room to room):

Northern Lights

Philip Pullman (1995)

Synopsis
Lyra's best friend is a boy named Roger Parslow, whose family works in the college. Together, the two of them plan adventures and battles. There is a rumour is going around Oxford that children are being stolen by a mysterious group called "the Gobblers." Soon after, Roger disappears.

Setting
A parallel universe, the Arctic

Themes
Innocence, morality, identity, fate vs. free will, deceit

Genre
Fantasy fiction

Page:

Read from:

AMBITION, CONFIDENCE, CREATIVITY, RESPECT, DETERMINATION

Proud to be part of:

For 25 minutes, every single child listened as their tutor read. Josie later explained that a Year 7 tutor group will read a minimum of 10 books a year; some will read 15. The books become more challenging and often lengthier higher up the school, but it is estimated that each child will read at least 25 books over their journey at Henley Bank. That is incredibly significant: 25 books at a time when it is becoming increasingly challenging to encourage reading for pleasure in young people. I believe this programme is responsible in part for Henley Bank's excellent results across all subject areas. GL Assessment's *Read All About It* report[84] highlights the correlation between poor reading skills and attainment across a range of subjects, with a stronger correlation in maths and science than in English literature.

84. GL Assessment. (2020) *Read All About It: why reading is key to GCSE success.* Retrieved from: www.gl-assessment.co.uk/whyreading (accessed 19.09.20)

Our visit was not just restricted to one corridor and we were able to see groups across the school. Those children considered the most challenging were some of the most engaged in the reading, and it was lovely to hear many of the books I enjoyed reading as a young person as I moved from room to room. Tutors were consistently confident and passionate in their storytelling, and that confidence and passion has clearly grown over time. Tutors carry out all the reading and the reasons for this were discussed in depth later in the day. As the adults in the room, tutors are best placed to convey the meaning within the text - their intonation and authority unlock the story in the most powerful way.

As part of the discussion, we had the chance to quiz Josie and Bradley on how they had created such an excellent system. The key points from the discussion are summarised here:

- The leadership team are deeply involved in the programme and leaders enjoy taking over the reading for each tutor group they visit.
- The programme runs from Years 7-11. Year 11 end their reading in January to switch to Tassomai and Hegarty Maths.
- Each school in the trust has a designated tutor reading programme lead within the leadership team, who spends time daily reading across tutor groups.
- Josie worked with MBE Books[85] to gain reasonable discounts on books (at Torquay Academy we have procured good-quality second-hand books from eBay and Amazon for around £2 each).
- During DEAR time (which happens every day for all year groups but Year 11), tutors read ahead in their tutor books and mark the tier 2 words, for which they will provide synonyms in the tutor reading time the next day.
- GL Assessment's New Group Reading Test (NGRT)[86] is administered at the start and end of each year for all year groups. This data has shown not just an improvement overall but also an improvement for those above-average students who score around 110 on standardised age scores - these scores often jump up to 130.
- There is an acknowledgement that reading is hard. Bradley discussed how he openly deciphers the meaning of challenging words in front of classes to show there is no shame in not knowing a word.

85. www.mbebooks.com
86. www.gl-assessment.co.uk/products/new-group-reading-test-ngrt

I thank Josie and Bradley for their generosity in sharing what is clearly working so exceptionally well at Henley Bank and across the Greenshaw Learning Trust. It is sharing such as this that is driving forward change across the educational landscape. People such as Josie and Bradley want to make a difference beyond their own school and trust because, in this case, they believe in the power of reading to improve the lives of young people.

Testing of reading ages

Schools take varying approaches to capturing data relating to reading ages. Some ask teachers to administer baseline tests in classrooms, some rely solely on KS2 data and others buy in standardised, computerised tests. How this data is used also varies from school to school. In this section I will outline an approach that quickly identifies those students most in need of additional support and monitors the progress of the cohort to ensure that issues can be addressed as they arise.

It is important that schools have a clear baseline of reading ages for their cohort that is independent from SATs results. Why? Well, a KS2 SATs paper is detailed and challenging; it covers a number of texts and uses a range of question formats. Some children are entitled to access arrangements to support them through the test, and primary schools take differing approaches to preparing students for the assessment. In addition, secondary schools do not receive the ratified results until later in the autumn term, and it is important to identify students who need support early on in the term.

There are a number of standardised reading age tests that can be used to provide a baseline. It is more expensive to purchase an online test, such as GL Assessment's NGRT, but it is quick and easy to administer and does not require marking. The test also provides data on a child's ability to comprehend texts at word and sentence level. Usually the scores are similar for both, but where there are differences it is useful to look more closely at the results to determine precisely the reading difficulty experienced by the child.

Age at test (yrs:mths)	SAS (90% confidence bands)		Overall stanine	NPR	GR (/259)	Reading age	Reading age confidence bands		Stanine	
		60 70 80 90 100					Lower	Upper	SC	PC
11:06	74		2	4	246	7:02	6:07	7:09	2	2
11:00	75		2	5	=244	7:01	6:06	7:08	3	1
11:09	72		1	3	249	6:11	6:04	7:06	2	1
11:08	73		1	4	=247	6:11	6:04	7:06	2	1
11:03	73		1	4	=247	6:10	6:03	7:05	1	1
11:05	71		1	3	250	6:07	6:00	7:02	2	1
11:09	69		1	2	=254	6:05	5:11	6:11	1	1
11:01	70		1	2	=251	6:04	5:10	6:10	2	1
11:00	70		1	2	=251	6:03	5:09	6:09	1	1
11:01	70		1	2	=251	6:02	5:08	6:08	3	1
11:10	69		1	2	=254	5:08	5:02	6:02	1	1
11:11	69		1	2	=254	5:01	4:07	5:07	1	1
11:04	69		1	2	=254	5:00-	5:00-	5:00-	1	-
11:05	69		1	2	=254	5:00-	5:00-	5:00-	1	-
11:11	69		1	2	=254	5:00-	5:00-	5:00-	1	-

Source: GL Assessment

The standardised age score (SAS) produced by the NGRT (see example above) is based on the results of the entire cohort of children who have taken the assessment nationally. Each child's result is weighted depending on their date of birth, so a child born later in the year will receive a scaled score. The SAS for the national cohort forms a bell curve, so a school is able to determine how their cohort compares with the national picture. Alongside the SAS, as discussed in chapter 1, each child is awarded a stanine for their word- and sentence-level comprehension. This indicates the section of the bell curve they are within.

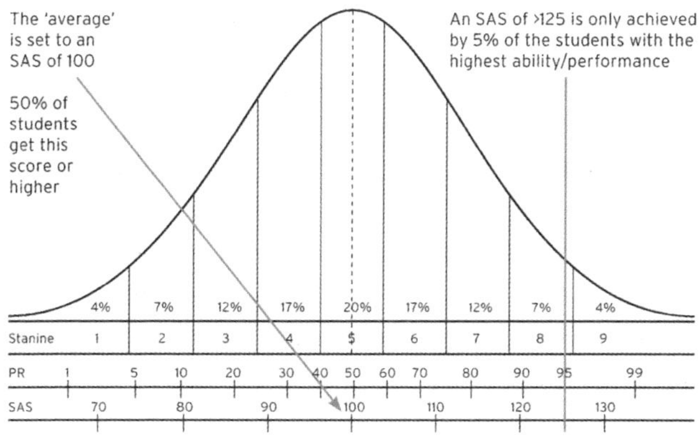

As a rule of thumb, any child with an SAS below 85-90 needs extra support. As outlined elsewhere in this book, extractions from lessons for reading intervention should only take place when absolutely necessary, so it is really important at this stage to triangulate the results and decide upon a personalised course of action for each child.

Triangulation of results

Once you have drawn up a list of the children with an SAS of less than 90, it is important to analyse these results alongside other data and information about each child. For Year 7s, primary schools will have provided data on SATs performance and softer data around attitude to learning, effort and behaviour, as well as pastoral information. For some children, it will be immediately obvious that their SAS does not chime with this information. Those children will need to be re-tested to find out if something happened to go wrong on the day – perhaps they took the test in a hurry or just didn't try very hard. Some students genuinely have low reading scores but cope very well in spite of this. As I will discuss in the next chapter, some have brilliant coping strategies and limiting their curriculum by extracting them for intervention is not always the best course of action. These children are likely to be willing to engage with after-school literacy support.

Reading interventions at King Alfred's Academy

I'm exceptionally grateful to Alice Visser-Furay, reading intervention specialist and literacy coordinator, who has spent many years building a reading culture at King Alfred's Academy in Wantage, Oxfordshire. Below, Alice sets out how she specifically targets students who are behind with their reading to support them to make good progress.

In order for interventions to be successful, a purposeful, systematic and personalised approach is essential. At King Alfred's Academy, the reading intervention specialist, the Accelerated Reader team leader and the SENCO begin by assessing who is behind with reading. This involves triangulating SATs results and personalised information about individual students from their primary school teachers (gathered in June for rising Year 7s) with Star Reading data from students' baseline test in September. Students who are one to two years behind their chronological age in reading are then put 'on watch'. Our experienced Accelerated Reader (AR) teachers focus on these students during the fortnightly structured silent reading lessons in classrooms, ensuring that they have books that interest and engage them. We are alert to the possibility of 'fake reading', so during AR lessons we ask students to note the page they started on at the beginning of the lesson and where they finished, and we look for patterns over time. In these lessons, we also check students' quizzing records: are they finishing books and successfully quizzing on them to show that they understand key ideas? All this leads to individual conversations with struggling students where we offer support to help them find books they will enjoy.

For reluctant readers, we have realised that short books that students can finish in one to two lessons are hugely beneficial in developing reading confidence and encouraging students to see themselves as readers. We buy books from Laburnum, Badger Learning and Barrington Stoke for this purpose. Many students have been 'switched on' to reading as a result of reading short books; several have ended up as word millionaires. AR teachers always have a supply of short books and popular reads with them in lessons, and they also have the possibility of sending students to the library to receive personalised guidance from our librarian.

For students more than two years behind with their reading, in addition to supporting them in AR lessons, we put more intensive interventions in place based on their individual needs. One-to-one sessions are the gold standard for effective interventions, according to Education Endowment Foundation research (2018), but they are also expensive. We decided to develop a team of a dozen trained community volunteers who provide one-to-one weekly 'reading partner' sessions for about 40 Year 7 and 8 students. Volunteers are assisted by the reading intervention specialist, who evaluates students to determine what the focus for the intervention should be: decoding, comprehension, fluency, vocabulary, EAL, building confidence or, most often, some combination of these. Intervention sessions take place in the library with the reading intervention specialist present to offer personalised advice for volunteers and students. This programme has been exceptionally effective, with students making on average 20 months' progress within seven months. It is heartwarming to see the grandparent-grandchild type of relationship that develops between volunteers and the students they work with, enabling students to have a positive experience of reading.

We have also developed a Reading Scholars programme for students in Years 7-10 who receive free school meals and are two or more years behind with their reading. This fortnightly intervention is run by trained pupil premium staff mentors using reciprocal reading strategies with non-fiction articles or extracts, mostly selected from the free site www.commonlit.org. Reciprocal reading improves comprehension by helping students to build their predicting, questioning, clarifying and summarising skills (EEF research indicates that the reciprocal reading approach is particularly useful for FSM-eligible students). Recently, we introduced this strategy to a group of a dozen Year 8 boys at risk of exclusion. These 'Link Leaders' participate in reciprocal reading sessions in small groups when they would have had French; the emphasis on complex tier 2 vocabulary in 'real world' articles is empowering for the boys, as they learn words like 'quantitative', 'adversity' and 'perilous', which other Year 8 students don't know. For these Link Leaders, we also set ambitious, personalised end-of-year word count goals in AR; this has proved highly motivating for students as they see their numbers increasing steadily (in fact, several of these Link Leaders have asked for their already ambitious targets to be increased).

Although we believe that 'in person' interventions with trained adults are most effective, together with the SEND department we offer electronic interventions as well, including Lexia PowerUp Literacy and recently ReadingWise; these differentiated web-based literacy instruction programmes focus on improving comprehension. We have also used Bedrock Vocabulary to good effect for some students – this online programme focuses on the tier 2 vocabulary that research shows is crucial for academic success. We have found that these programmes work best when students use them regularly (ideally on a daily basis) with adult support, encouragement and careful scrutiny. Communication with parents about how these interventions should be used at home is vital.

We monitor the reading progress of KS3 students through Star Reading tests four times a year and also utilise feedback from parents and teachers. At-risk students are checked during KS4 to ensure that they leave King Alfred's fully literate. We have a 'never give up' approach to students who are behind with their reading: if an intervention doesn't seem to be having an impact, the reading intervention specialist has a one-to-one conversation with the student to explore barriers so that we can try a different approach.

Our library is dynamic, with a wide range of diverse books to appeal to students and many activities to foster a buzz around reading. We also work hard to provide students with books of their own at home; we buy large numbers of books from charity shops that are gifted to students or sold at a low cost during parents' evenings (50p per book). Communication with home is important for success, so we explain to parents what interventions are being put in place for their child, and offer practical and tailored suggestions about how parents might bolster reading progress. Overall, we believe strongly in the need for personalised support for students, rather than a blanket 'one size fits all' approach.

Developing a writing culture

Most schools would say they aspire to create a reading culture and it has a central position in their wider school aims. But it is not often that we extend this same focus to creating a writing culture. Although many teachers would identify reading as an enjoyable pastime, writing often comes to be associated with hard work – painstaking essay or dissertation writing, for example – and more functional tasks such as writing letters or emails to parents. Writing is not often associated with pleasure and we signal this attitude to the children in our care. Students frequently used to arrive in my classroom asking 'Is there much writing today?' because they had negative associations with writing.

How I responded to that question changed over time. I realised that if I apologetically explained that, yes, today we would be writing up paragraphs – or that, no, today we would be focusing on reading – I was feeding into a culture of negativity around writing. It has now been a few years since I have been asked this question. Students have come to understand that, yes, there will always be a fair amount of writing in the lesson, but that this writing will be appropriately scaffolded and achievable. It won't always be easy: students will be introduced to challenging concepts, but they will usually connect to prior knowledge and be applied using familiar sentence stems. For example, we might look at the concept of hubris, applying it to the familiar character of Mr Birling in *An Inspector Calls* and then more broadly to the Edwardian bourgeoisie.

For a teacher, there is nothing better than the feeling that comes when children are proud of the writing they have done and happy to show it off. Part of our job as educators is to ensure that all children are given the opportunity to perceive themselves in more 'intellectual' roles. The fresh start offered by secondary school is a chance for young people to reinvent themselves in this capacity. Clearly, this is easier in some subjects than others, but at Torquay Academy almost every lesson starts with a silent written activity (usually retrieval practice). In every subject there is an expectation that writing will take place; the familiarity of this routine has removed much of the fear that leads to questions like 'Is there much writing today?'

Why were those children so concerned about writing? Perhaps, for them, writing had always been associated with failure. Perhaps their writing had been criticised for spelling and punctuation errors to such an extent that they viewed themselves as 'bad writers'. As set out in chapter 1, there are two ways to avoid this feeling of failure. First, ensure children have a clear understanding of key concepts by creating a knowledge-rich curriculum. Second, explicitly model tasks that are then scaffolded for independence. The more opportunities children have to practise writing across the disciplines, the less it will be viewed as something to be feared and failed at. They can start to perceive writing as achievable and an opportunity to show off how much they have learned. For more guidance on improving writing across a school community, Judith Hochman and Natalie Wexler's *The Writing Revolution*[87] is an invaluable resource that I can't recommend highly enough.

87. Hochman, JC and Wexler, N. (2017) *The Writing Revolution*, Jossey-Bass

Writing as a source of power

If we consider those who are in a position of power in society, it is obvious that writing has aided their success. Even if we remove the requirement to write in order to access higher education, and consider those who have derided the importance of education in achieving success, none would deny that their ability to write has been central to that success. For Richard Branson to build his business empire, he needed to write detailed business plans and proposals. Jeremy Clarkson regularly reminds A-level students of his results (a C and 2 Us) and how they didn't hold him back, but he is a broadcaster who regularly writes columns and articles to further his career.

If we feed into young people's self-narratives by limiting the amount they are expected to write if they find it difficult, we are ultimately limiting their ability to go on and gain power within society. How many young people have we met who appear confident and articulate, have the charm and charisma that makes them popular with their peers, but the minute they are asked to put pen to paper they either misbehave or put their head on the desk? These young people have leadership potential that could be put to positive use in their communities, but their fear of writing (so often perceived as laziness) will hold them back.

There are many subjects where students with weaker literacy skills thrive because, particularly at KS3, in theory a unit can be taught without much reading and writing. I think it is really important that children have access to this varied curriculum, and I certainly would not expect them to spend all day writing at desks. However, it is important that the lack of writing is not celebrated. To build a culture that values writing, it is important that teachers discuss the writing tasks that might be involved if students wish to pursue a career in this subject, and do not associate a child's success in their subject with the reduced requirement to write.

Writing as catharsis

There is a correlation between those children with weaker literacy skills and those who have had adverse childhood experiences (ACEs). A significant amount of research has taken place into writing as a means of gradually easing trauma. Therefore, there is potentially a double benefit to be gained from integrating writing into programmes such as Thrive[88] that are specifically aimed at children who have experienced trauma. This can help children to view writing positively, as well as providing a powerful means of therapy.

In Pennebaker and Beall's original study of the effect of writing about traumatic events,[89] it was important that participants did not worry about spelling, punctuation and grammar, and I think this is vital in altering a child's attitude towards writing. Fear that they will spell a word incorrectly or misplace a comma can hold a child back from writing at all. Certainly, when it comes to writing about trauma, any adult involved in the process must not view it as an opportunity to critique or provide feedback. Rather, it is a chance for young people to find their voices through writing and to experience writing as a positive means of self-expression. Ultimately, in an educational context, all our subjects are geared towards this. If a child enters further academic study of any subject, they will need to express their views in an extended written format. If they start to build their confidence in writing in Year 7, this will provide a powerful basis for further academic study.

A note on SPAG

Spelling, punctuation and grammar are undoubtedly important to get right. Their assessment has been introduced to subjects beyond English in recent years, in an attempt to elevate their status. However, a relentless focus on SPAG in every subject at all times is likely to do more harm than good for students with weaker literacy skills. It can also consume a disproportionate amount of teachers' time: many schools have introduced policies that require SPAG marking in all subjects, including maths, even when feedback in other areas is more likely to help a child progress.

88. www.thriveapproach.com
89. Pennebaker, JW and Beall, SK. (1986) 'Confronting a traumatic event: toward an understanding of inhibition and disease', *Journal of Abnormal Psychology*, 95:3, pp.274-81

If a child has produced a successful piece of writing that expresses their ideas clearly but has the odd spelling or punctuation error, then by all means identify the errors if there will be an opportunity for the child to make corrections. But if a child has struggled over a piece of work, underlining and correcting every sentence is likely to be demotivational, particularly if they will have no chance to learn from the mistakes.

For children with weaker literacy skills, it is far preferable to help them avoid making these mistakes in the first place. Providing word banks of key vocabulary and sentence stems to aid the structure of writing will ensure that students regularly practise their use of more challenging vocabulary and ultimately rely on those scaffolds less and less. Learning to spell is not about continually having your mistakes circled in work that is handed back – this will just reinforce feelings of writing failure. Dr Margaret Peters devised the 'look, cover, write, check' approach to teaching spelling; she argued that the belief that children would pick up spellings from reading or listening was unhelpful, and that more explicit approaches were necessary. Her book *Spelling: Caught or Taught?*[90] advocated the 'taught' method: the explicit teaching of key word spellings, alongside regular practice, as opposed to assuming that children's spelling will improve if inaccuracies are 'caught' and pointed out within a piece of writing.

In an ideal world, children will use vocabulary banks as a reference point but will not copy directly from them. Rather, they should look at the word, cover it, attempt to spell it from memory, then check their spelling. This memorisation is crucial in the long term, but some children will need more support than others in reaching that point. Our SENDCo at Torquay Academy, Eloise Jukes, suggests that it can be empowering to allow children to point out their own spelling uncertainties: once they have finished writing, they can circle those words they are unsure of. This is an invitation to the teacher to support their correction of the word, or provide reassurance that their spelling is accurate.

90. Peters, ML. (1985) *Spelling: Caught or Taught?*, Routledge

Chapter 17. From a whole-school approach to a personalised approach

A report from the Joseph Rowntree Foundation, *Special Educational Needs and Their Links to Poverty*,[91] includes some stark figures that show disadvantaged children are more likely to be diagnosed with SEND and more likely to have lower attainment and literacy levels.

Percentage of children experiencing income poverty over time by SEND status

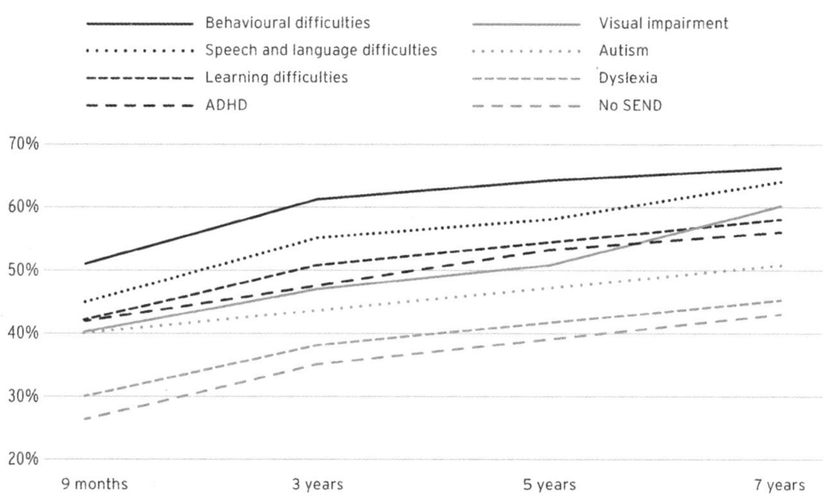

Note: income poverty is usually defined as less than 60% of median income.

Source: Joseph Rowntree Foundation

91. Shaw, B, Bernardes, E, Trethewey, A and Menzies, L. (2016) *Special Educational Needs and Their Links to Poverty*, Joseph Rowntree Foundation. Retrieved from: https://www.jrf.org.uk/file/48923/download?token=3DkPP-d0&filetype=full-report (accessed 19.09.20)

According to the Joseph Rowntree Foundation (JRF), the proportion of children with SEND who are living in poverty increases with age for all types of SEND. What are the reasons for this? First, children who live in poverty are more likely than their affluent peers to develop some forms of SEND, such as behavioural difficulties, as they experience 'persistently challenging family circumstances'. Second, the families of children with SEND are more likely to move into poverty (for example, as a result of the costs and/or family stress associated with their child's SEND status).

The most effective ways to support disadvantaged pupils' achievement

1. **Whole-school ethos of attainment for all:** schools have an ethos of high attainment for all pupils and avoid stereotyping disadvantaged pupils as all facing similar barriers or having less potential to succeed.

2. **Addressing behaviour and attendance:** schools ensure effective behaviour strategies are in place, respond quickly to poor attendance and provide strong social and emotional support, including through working with families.

3. **High-quality teaching for all:** schools emphasise 'quality teaching first' and provide consistently high standards by setting expectations, monitoring performance and sharing best practice.

4. **Meeting individual learning needs:** staff identify each pupil's challenges and interests. They seek the best strategies to help each pupil make the next step in their learning. Schools provide individual support for specific learning needs and group support for pupils with similar needs.

5. **Deploying staff effectively:** schools devolve responsibility to frontline staff, use their best teachers to work with pupils who need the most support and train teaching assistants to support pupils' learning.

6. **Data-driven and responding to evidence:** teachers use data to identify pupils' learning needs, review progress every few weeks and address underperformance quickly. They have manageable Assessment for Learning systems, which provide clear feedback for pupils. Schools use evidence to make decisions about their support strategies.

7. **Clear, responsive leadership:** Senior leaders set ever higher aspirations and lead by example. They hold all their staff accountable for raising attainment, rather than accepting low aspirations and variable performance. They share their thinking and invest in staff training.

Source: National Foundation for Educational Research/Department for Education

In terms of breaking the link between SEND and poverty, a key recommendation of the JRF report is to move 'towards a model where children with SEND in mainstream schools have their needs met first and foremost by their class or subject teacher, with more specialist provision used where appropriate'. This chimes with research undertaken by the National Foundation for Educational Research, which identified seven building blocks common in schools that are more successful in raising disadvantaged students' attainment (see opposite).[92]

The idea that all children benefit from effective teaching is unsurprising, as is the level of impact that an effective teacher can have on learning for all students, including for those who are disadvantaged and/or have SEND. The first chapter of this book outlines the strategies that are likely to have the most impact on students, so I will not repeat those ideas here. Rather, I will consider some of the special educational needs that children, particularly those with lower literacy levels, may be diagnosed with. I will outline specific ways in which those strategies from chapter 1 can benefit children with the particular need, alongside other ways of providing a more personalised approach.

It is important to recognise the complexity behind the diagnosis of a particular special educational need. Many of the apparent symptoms of autism, for example, can present themselves as a result of trauma. Meeting the needs of children who have had adverse childhood experiences (ACEs) can be challenging and complicated, and the correlation between ACEs and poor literacy is stark. Schools should make effective use of educational psychologists, who can offer expert advice on the strategies most likely to be effective with individual children, particularly if they struggle in calm and structured classroom environments where their literacy needs are supported.

92. National Foundation for Educational Research/Department for Education. (2015) 'What are the most effective ways to support disadvantaged pupils' achievement?' Retrieved from: http://torview.org/file/10674 (accessed 19.09.20)

Dyslexia or visual stress

The symptoms of dyslexia differ from person to person, but they can include:

- Difficulties with reading and spelling.
- Visual disturbances when reading.
- Poor short-term memory.
- Organisational difficulties.

It is important to point out that there is no relationship between dyslexia and ability. Many children have developed excellent coping strategies that mean their dyslexia does not act as a barrier to learning. You may only notice their dyslexia in their spelling, which in and of itself will not necessarily prevent them from achieving highly. However, it will hold them back if their spelling is overly scrutinised and they are made to feel they are 'bad' at writing because they struggle with spelling (see page 186 for further details on SPAG).

Children with dyslexia are likely to benefit from an environment where copying from the board is limited and printed copies are available if PowerPoint is used.[93] This can be achieved through providing workbooks or booklets to all children. Dyslexia is a spectrum and there may well be children with undiagnosed dyslexic traits who will also benefit significantly from a dyslexia-friendly classroom.

Children with dyslexia may need additional thinking time before being asked to respond to a question. Thinking time is essential for all children and should correspond to the complexity of the question. There could be a few moments of silence before children are called upon to answer, or children could be asked to bullet-point their ideas before responding. Alternatively, they could be asked to discuss their thoughts briefly with a partner before giving their answer to the class.

93. MacKay, N. (2006) *Removing Dyslexia as a Barrier to Achievement: the dyslexia friendly schools toolkit*, SEN Marketing

A personalised approach

- A child with dyslexia may need additional time to complete tasks. Before the lesson, ensure you have identified the most fundamental written tasks that must be completed and prioritise these for children with dyslexia if necessary.
- A child with dyslexia may struggle with personal organisation. As mentioned previously, workbooks or booklets can help with this in class. For homework, provide a clear structure that focuses on retrieval practice, as described in chapter 1. Staff who support children with dyslexia at school will then have a clear idea of how to support them with their homework; this clarity will also be useful for parents when supporting their child at home.
- A child with dyslexia will particularly benefit from access to the key words they struggle to spell. Vocabulary banks for current topics, knowledge organisers and dictionaries are valuable tools to support the memorisation of key spellings.

Attention deficit hyperactivity disorder

The most common type of ADHD is combined ADHD, which involves the following symptoms:

- Constant motion, including squirming and fidgeting.
- Not listening/appearing not to be listening.
- Interrupting others/excessive talking.
- Being easily distracted and leaving tasks unfinished.
- Difficulties with working memory and longer-term retention.

Children with ADHD, as with all children, are likely to benefit from a structured learning environment with well-organised and established routines and clear behaviour expectations. A silent start to the lesson with predictable retrieval practice can provide a calm and non-threatening environment in which they feel safe. Setting clear expectations is the first step in facilitating success for a child with ADHD, as they understand exactly what they need to do. This is particularly powerful if the expectations and routines are consistent across the school.

A personalised approach

- Children with ADHD will particularly benefit from being 'caught' doing something right. Warm and meaningful praise for early success – made possible through clear expectations and achievable tasks – will lay strong foundations for that lesson and for a positive relationship with the child.
- Children with ADHD will benefit from the assumption of innocence. Instead of taking an accusatory tone, particularly with the first infraction, talking about what you want to see can have a greater impact. For example, rather than saying, 'Stop staring out of the window or you won't understand what's going on', a simple 'Show me you are listening' reframes your request for attention positively.
- There is a whole range of de-escalation techniques that are particularly powerful for those with ADHD. I would recommend Doug Lemov's *Teach Like a Champion*[94] as a starting point for strategies that will benefit the whole class but will disproportionately benefit students with ADHD, owing to the focus on clear expectations combined with positive reinforcement.

Autism spectrum condition

Although autism is officially classed as a spectrum 'disorder', the infinitely preferable term is 'condition' and that is what will be used here. There are three functional levels of autism:[95]

- **Level 1: requires support**. Difficulty initiating social interactions; organisation and planning problems can hamper independence.

94. Lemov, D. (2015) *Teach Like a Champion 2.0*, Jossey-Bass
95. Rudy, LJ. (2019) 'What are the 3 levels of autism?', *Verywell Health*. Retrieved from: www.verywellhealth.com/what-are-the-three-levels-of-autism-260233 (accessed 19.09.20)

- **Level 2: requires substantial support.** Social interactions are limited to narrow special interests; frequent restricted/repetitive behaviours.
- **Level 3: requires very substantial support.** Severe deficits in verbal and non-verbal social communication skills; great distress/difficulty in changing actions or focus.

In a mainstream school environment, we may teach children with level 1 or 2 ASC. Children within level 3 have very specialist requirements in terms of support and are also likely to have other health needs. It is unlikely their needs will be met in a mainstream setting, therefore this section will focus on children whose condition is within levels 1 and 2.

Many of the symptoms of autism can be applied to all children to some extent, and not all children with ASC will have all the common traits. An ASC-friendly environment will therefore benefit all children. It is of primary importance to have a calm, well-ordered, routine-based learning environment in which children with ASC feel safe and secure. Anxiety can be aroused by even small emotional triggers, such as a negative comment made by another student in the corridor or as they enter the classroom. A teacher's presence at the door as students arrive ensures a calm start to the lesson and minimises opportunities for negative social interactions. Children with ASC can misinterpret social cues or comments, and can also react to them in ways that other students find amusing or frustrating. Some young people will look for ways to provoke reactions in children with ASC, and these reactions can derail the start of a lesson for them and others. Prevention is better than cure, so it is particularly important for teachers of children with ASC to be well prepared for the lesson and the arrival of their students.

It's a myth that children with ASC are not able to form social relationships; the reverse is true. A child with ASC is likely to be particularly attuned to the behaviour of others towards them, even if they are then prone to misinterpret this behaviour. It is essential, therefore, to give children with ASC – and all children, for that matter – a warm and heartfelt welcome as they arrive in class. They need to know you are happy to see them and look forward to teaching them, despite what may have taken place in the previous lesson. Getting to know the child and building a relationship with them is so important for those who struggle with social interactions.

A personalised approach

- Work to build positive relationships with children who have ASC. Ensure they are welcomed at the start of the lesson, along with others in the class.
- Ensure that routines are well established. When an ASC child has a teaching assistant or needs to be sat in a particular area of the room, make sure the arrangements are in place.
- Support personal organisation by giving low-level reminders of the materials that students need in front of them. De-escalation techniques are really important: a quiet reminder, a walk away, a circle back if needed. Personal organisation can also be supported through the use of booklets or workbooks, alongside clarity regarding homework.
- Break tasks down and explicitly model each stage. Ensure that independent tasks are scaffolded appropriately.
- A child with ASC may need additional time to complete tasks. Before the lesson, ensure you have identified the most fundamental written tasks that must be completed and prioritise these for children with ASC if necessary.

Acknowledgements

On a personal note

There are so many people to thank for their expertise and input to this book, but I would like to start these acknowledgements with a personal story. It is a comparison of two different educational experiences – a comparison that I believe illustrates how life chances can be determined not by intelligence or potential, but by expectations.

I was brought up in a family that was by no means affluent, but my parents had jobs that covered the bills and they put money aside for a holiday now and again. I had cousins and uncles who went to university and although my parents didn't go on to higher education, I knew that I would have this opportunity if I wished – there was always talk of a savings account 'for university'. I attended a comprehensive school that had its share of problems and I am not going to say my time there was perfect. But I understood where my qualifications would lead, I knew the value of education and my mum was a brilliant role model for reading. I will never be able to express how grateful I am to my parents for the strong, supportive and loving start to life that led me to believe there was a place in the academic world for me if I chose to take it.

My husband's contrasting educational experience really sparked my interest in the issues discussed in this book. He was brought up in an equally loving home where, again, higher education was not the norm. His entitlement to free school meals never meant that he went without, and his mum took pride in making sure he was well turned out and always arrived at school on time. His role models were hardworking people who left school as soon as possible to start earning a living. When we started dating 20 years ago, there was a mis-match between the articulate, curious and perceptive young man that I knew and the person who was crippled with anxiety when it came to writing a letter and completely clueless when it came to understanding the 39.9% APR on his credit card statement.

He hadn't hated school, it had just seemed a bit pointless. He had no intrinsic motivation to study in order to attain qualifications and he never had any sense that his teachers believed he could achieve anything. He talked about being in the bottom set, never being chased for homework – just coasting along and putting pen to paper as little as possible. His school had a reasonable reputation, but he was essentially invisible there.

I convinced him to go back to college after we had been together for a short while; they required a list of his previous qualifications in order to begin an access course. I will never forget the moment I opened the letter from his school's exams officer, which listed his results: FFEGFGGF. As someone who placed such value on education, I just couldn't comprehend how this had happened – he was so knowledgeable and perceptive about the world, so articulate on so many topics. To my naive and inexperienced mind, it just didn't make any sense. I had thought that people who failed their exams just weren't that clever, but this was shaking my view of the world. What if people who didn't get qualifications *were* clever, but didn't always make the best choices when they were at school, because they were *children*. What could my husband have achieved if his teachers had expected more of him? Is there even such a thing as being 'clever', or is the key to success a positive, challenging, stimulating educational experience that, unfortunately, not every child has access to?

The 'cleverness' of my husband was 'proven' when he graduated from university with a computer science degree and went on to become a software engineer. The lines of code he has to write in order for a program to operate are far beyond my comprehension. He writes detailed reports, chairs meetings, gives presentations to stakeholders – things he had always been capable of. When I look at the students in my classes who aren't doing their best, who don't want to try, who try to get away with doing the minimum, I see my husband as a schoolboy and I try to be the teacher he didn't have. The teacher who says, 'I know you and you can do better than this.'

My brilliant colleagues

After reading this book, you will understand the significant impact that my principal at Torquay Academy, Steve Margetts, has had on its direction. I am indebted to him for the time and energy he has put into researching what works for disadvantaged learners and how to create a school where they can thrive.

I also have the privilege of working with my sister, Eloise Jukes, who has been a further source of inspiration for me. Her own educational path was not as straightforward as mine and her achievement in overcoming those barriers was phenomenal. As SENDCo at a school with almost 1500 students, she works tirelessly to provide them with the support they need to access the curriculum. I am incredibly grateful that she never gets bored of talking about teaching and that her role aligns so closely with my own in literacy. Many of the literacy interventions established at our school were originally put in place by Eloise and she provided invaluable support in putting together chapter 17.

Writing the maths and science chapters of this book posed the greatest challenge for me and I am extremely grateful for the support of Mark Gale and Owen Gratton. They politely corrected my inaccuracies/misconceptions and provided excellent suggestions for further reading. Most of all, they were kind about what I was trying to achieve and gave invaluable support and encouragement.

My colleagues in the English department are a constant source of expert subject knowledge and are absolutely driven to deliver a curriculum that provides all our students with the opportunity to reach academic excellence. Jen Brimming, Jamie Engineer and Karen Elson have provided wonderful resources that are shared among the whole team and our department meetings are totally focused on preparing to deliver curriculum content in the most effective ways. I'm privileged to work with every single member of our team.

It has been incredibly rewarding to work with Harrison Littler and Natalie Jones on developing our coaching programme and our 'blueprint for teaching and learning'. Identifying our core teaching principles provided many lightbulb moments that connect to literacy, specifically how each teacher can adapt the modelling process to provide instruction in reading and writing within their discipline. I am also blessed to work with Carol Rowan, the driving force behind the second draft of the TA Dictionary; she worked tirelessly (and endlessly) to research the etymology of thousands of words and present them in an accessible format. She is so driven and passionate about improving the literacy skills of our young people and we are lucky to have her.

Our librarian, Charlotte Aitken, has an encyclopedic knowledge of young adult fiction; she has worked so hard to introduce Accelerated Reader and to support and encourage students with their reading. She has also developed our vocabulary Tassomai – based on key words from the TA Dictionary as well as common word roots, prefixes and suffixes – so that students are quizzed regularly on these key terms.

The wider educational community

I am particularly grateful to Andy Buck, not only for the support and encouragement he has provided in the writing of this book, but also for the CPD he has delivered at Torquay Academy over the past five years. He has brought key leadership research into the development of our strategic aims. His one-to-one coaching sessions are also invaluable in asking those challenging questions that are crucial to self-reflection.

Alex Quigley is a hero of the literacy community, bringing literacy and explicit vocabulary teaching to the forefront of the minds of school leaders at such a crucial time. I am so grateful for his kindness and generosity in agreeing to write the foreword to this book.

Alice Visser-Furay is equally heroic in her passion and commitment not only to improve the literacy skills of children at her own school, but also children in schools across the country, where literacy coordinators are inspired by her work. Her knowledge of literacy is second to none; her generosity of spirit in sharing her expertise is mirrored in the generosity of the @Team_English1 community on Twitter, to whom I am also indebted.

I am grateful to Kat Howard, Adam Boxer, Gemma Scott, Dawn Cox and Andy Prestoe for their subject knowledge and expertise, and to all the teachers at Michaela Community School for writing so comprehensively about the knowledge-rich curriculum they offer. Thank you also to Josie Mingay at Henley Bank High School, for introducing visitors to your tutor reading programme and for being kind enough to allow me to write about it. I would not have been able to write this book without drawing heavily on the knowledge and expertise of other practitioners and I am eternally grateful for their generosity.

The publishing team

Thank you to Alex Sharratt for believing in the concept, and to him and Jonathan Barnes for providing encouragement and support right from the start. Thank you to Isla McMillan for her patience and kind words when I needed them, and for the brilliant job she has done throughout the editing process. I am indebted to everyone at John Catt for bringing to life a project that I feel I've been working on since the start of my career.